# BRAINSTORM!

## The Stories of Twenty American Kid Inventors

## TOM TUCKER

### With drawings by Richard Loehle

A Sunburst Book
Farrar, Straus and Giroux

Distributed in Canada by Douglas & McIntyre Ltd.
Printed in May 2010 in the United States of America
by RR Donnelley & Sons Company, Harrisonburg, Virginia
First edition, 1995
Sunburst edition, 1998
20   19   18   17   16   15   14

Library of Congress Cataloging-in-Publication Data
Tucker, Tom.
    Brainstorm! : the stories of twenty American kid inventors /
Tom Tucker ; with drawings by Richard Loehle. — 1st ed.
        p.   cm.
    ISBN: 978-0-374-40928-9 (pbk.)
    Includes bibliographical references (p.   ).
    1. Children as inventors—United States—Biography—Juvenile
literature.   2. Inventions—United States—History—Juvenile
literature.   [1. Children as inventors.   2. Inventors.
3. Inventions.]   I. Loehle, Richard, ill.   II. Title.

T39.T85   1995
 609.2'273— dc20

                                    94-38780

# ACKNOWLEDGMENTS

Covering more than two hundred years of American history, this book takes a look at some of the surprising inventions that have come from young people ranging in age from five to nineteen. I could not possibly have assembled this project without the generous assistance of a number of inventors, of their friends and relatives and descendants, and of numerous individuals and institutions whose help and generosity were sometimes as startling and unforeseen as the inventors' stories themselves. If I forget to thank anyone here, it is unintentional.

I owe a great debt to the inventors from the present day, who were patient with my interviews: Hannah Cannon, Al Glover, Vanessa Hess, Beatrice Kenner, Maurice Scales, Becky Schroeder, Mary Spaeth, and Jerrald Spencer.

As indicated in my source notes, many relatives, descendants, teachers, associates, and friends of the inventors in this book shared their knowledge, and I thank them all.

George Epperson kindly permitted me access to family papers and memorabilia relating to his father's invention, which made it possible to write the history of the Popsicle. In addition, John Epperson and Leo Epperson provided assistance.

I am very grateful to two authors who have also written books about inventors: Anne Macdonald, who throughout this effort shared her knowledge and her wise and sympathetic advice; and Steven Caney, who gave me access to his Chester Greenwood sources.

My searches have been aided by many research specialists, including Polly Boggess, Mary Gene Dykes, and Marcelle White of the Whitfield-Murray Historical Society in Dalton, Georgia; Marion Canedo; Ms. St. Julien R. Childs of the South Carolina Historical Society; Sarah Griswold and Mary Harwood of the Historical Museum of the Gunn Memorial Library in Washington, Connecticut; Patricia Hardin of Norris Public Library in Rutherfordton, North Carolina; Portia James of the Smithsonian Institution; Patricia Ives Sluby of the U.S. Patent and Trademark Office; Autumn Stanley, author of *Mothers and Daughters of Invention* (Rutgers, 1995); Martha Taylor, licensed patent agent; John Warren; and Cathryn Wilson of the Maine State Library. I also thank the following researchers: Matthew Tucker, Jennifer Mayhew, and Joseph Tucker.

I have depended on many libraries in addition to those mentioned above and these include: Chicago Public Library; Chicago Historical Society Library; University of North Carolina at Chapel Hill Library; Duke University libraries; Oakland Public Library; Anne Kent California History Room of the Marin County Free Library, San Rafael, California; Glencoe (Illinois) Public Library; Greenville County (South Carolina) Public Library; the New York City Public Library; Dalton (Georgia) Library; Charleston Historical Society Library; Charleston Library Society; Charleston Public Library; Framingham (Massachusetts) Public Library; Spartanburg County (South Carolina) Library; Cook Memorial Library, Libertyville, Illinois; and the National Archives, Washington, D.C. I am grateful to

Michael Greene of the Isothermal Community College Library at Spindale, North Carolina, for obtaining materials for me at a remote rural site through interlibrary loan.

I received kind assistance from the American Water Ski Association, Chrysler Corporation, Gold Bond–Good Humor Ice Cream, Steven Manufacturing, Thomson Consumer Electronics, and Westinghouse Electric.

Whatever I needed at the U.S. Patent and Trademark Office was always provided, through the graces of Oscar Mastin. Project XL of the Patent and Trademark Office and Jerry Green at Invent America! also supplied invaluable assistance.

In putting this into final form, I owe much to my editor, Wes Adams, and his assistants, Elizabeth Mikesell and Laura Tillotson, not only in literary matters but in research support that went far beyond the call of duty.

# CONTENTS

⚡ CONTENTS

# BRAINSTORM!

*The Yankee boy, before he's sent to school,*
*Well knows the mystery of that magic tool,*
*. . . by his genius and his jack-knife driven,*
*Ere long he'll solve you any problem given.*
                    —J. PIERPONT, Massachusetts, 1857

*The great difference between young America and Old Fogy, is*
*the result of Discoveries, Inventions, and Improvements.*
                    —ABRAHAM LINCOLN, Illinois, 1859

*The first thing you want in a new country, is a patent office.*
                    —MARK TWAIN, Connecticut, 1889

*It just popped into my mind. I get lots of little ideas.*
                    —HANNAH CANNON, California, 1992

# INTRODUCTION

**Y**oung or old, most inventors are thrilled when they see their name on a patent issued by the United States Patent and Trademark Office in Arlington, Virginia, near Washington, D.C. In 1790, one Samuel Hopkins of Pittsford, Vermont, was granted the first U.S. patent, for an improvement in the making of potash (a substance derived from the ash of burned plant life and used to make soap and other items). The reviewer of this patent was Thomas Jefferson, the Secretary of State and himself an inventor, whose work area was filled with gadgets he had devised (perhaps he examined the patent on the famous portable desk that he invented in 1775). Jefferson next passed the document to the Secretary of War for his review and then obtained signatures from the Attorney General and, finally, from President Washington.

So began something bigger than the Founding Fathers had ever dreamed. During that first year, Jefferson received two more patent applications, both of which were granted after due deliberation and signature-collecting. But sometime during 1791, as he scrutinized models and sorted through stacks of designs, Jefferson realized that patent-examining was too much for busy Cabinet members. For as little as four dollars, American inventors could seek patent protection for their inventions under provisions of the Act of 1790. And seek it they did.

Jefferson found himself overwhelmed by an outpouring of American inventiveness. By 1793, patent-examining duties had been reassigned to a State Department clerk, until the Patent Office was formed in 1802. Today there are more than eight million patents that have been issued to Americans and other nationals by the U.S. Patent and Trademark Office.

A patent is a unique government document. According to Article 1, Section 8, of the United States Constitution, signed in Philadelphia in 1787: "The Congress shall have Power . . . to promote the Progress of Science and useful Arts, by securing for limited Times to Authors and Inventors the exclusive Right to their respective Writings and Discoveries." Basically, a patent is a contract between an inventor and the public: the inventor discloses the details of his or her invention, and, in exchange, the government, on behalf of the people, awards a monopoly, or exclusive right, on selling or making a profit from the invention for the period of the patent. For many years, the time limit on a patent was seventeen years from when the patent was granted. In our era, it has been changed to twenty years from when a patent application is filed. Although the U.S. government generally prohibits monopolies—no one company is allowed to take over the soft-drink business, for example—a patent is a monopoly that is legal.

Why give inventors this special advantage? It is a trade-off that benefits everyone. After the patent expires, industries may develop by using the invention without licensing cost. Before that expiration date, the inventor reaps the profits.

When an application arrives at the Patent Office, no one knows whether a patent will be granted—not until the examiner who specializes in that product field studies the application and reaches a conclusion. This decision is based on several factors.

First, is the invention new? If the examiner finds that no one has disclosed the invention previously, the first hurdle is overcome. Few inventions are totally new. Many patents are granted on ideas that are improvements on existing inventions. However, the examiner will not grant patents which embody only slight alterations.

Second, is the invention useful? The examiners view this issue leniently—how something may be used is not always apparent at the outset.

Third, does the invention work? In the nineteenth century, the Patent Office required three-dimensional models to prove the point. Nowadays, a two-dimensional ink drawing will suffice, but if rival inventors claim the same invention at the same time, the patent may go to the inventor who first built a working model.

Finally, is the patent claim well defined? The *words* of the application can be as important as the drawing, or even the *idea*. The language in the application must not be too broad and claim too much, or too narrow and claim too little. A lawyer's expertise comes in handy here. The application must also describe clearly how to make and use the invention.

No one knows for sure how many patents have been issued to kids. The granting of a patent is a no-nonsense process that doesn't require the applicant to state age, sex, race, or nationality. In our time, a patent examiner realized that one inventor, Robert Patch, might be a child because, although he had successfully designed a new toy truck, he had to use an X to sign his name. It turns out he was six years old. In my research, I've come across a few other very young inventors:

*In 1978, six-year-old Alex Z. Gustafson of Chicago noticed a sparkling effect when fragments of a crayon containing glitter dropped into the melting wax of candles on his birthday cake. The result? He thought up a "molten wax decoration," which was later awarded patent #4,419,070.*

*One day in 1989, Jim Leas was holding his four-month-old daughter Zoe, when she grabbed a mobile, let it go, and then caught it when it swung back. This led to "Baby Ball," a toy that was awarded patent #5,135,233. "Just the fact that she played with the mobile showed me it was a toy," said the father, who put his daughter's name on the patent.*

*In 1986, six-year-old Bettie Levy designed a board game, with some help from her parents, who are professional game designers. She now has it nationally marketed by the Ungame Company of California.*

Some observers are a bit skeptical of these "extra-young" inventors, noting heavy parental involvement. But what's wrong with a parent-child team arriving at a great idea together? Or what about a parent-child-dog team?

*When she was seven, Betty Galloway of Georgetown, South Carolina, began playing with a piece of wood chewed on by her dog, Caesar. She discovered it made a great bath toy. Her father, James, saw possibilities, too, and started a commercial venture based on the toy. On August 6, 1968, Betty received patent #3,395,481.*

———

Jefferson had no idea what was developing the first year he screened patent applications for the United States government. The flood of ideas, from young and old alike, had just begun.

# CHESTER GREENWOOD
## THE BOY BEHIND THE FLAP

It all started with ears, Chester Greenwood's ears. Chester's ears got cold. They got so cold something had to be done. That something was an invention by a fifteen-year-old boy that would support him for the rest of his life. The invention? Earmuffs.

Later, when Chester Greenwood had become a legend, newspaper writers started the story that his ears turned weird colors in the cold. According to *The Wall Street Journal*, "Chester Greenwood's ears were so sensitive that they turned chalky white, beet red, and deep blue (in that order) when the mercury dipped." Talk to the Greenwood descendants and the facts of the matter are different. What was wrong with Chester's ears?

"Just cold," says grandson George Greenwood. "Big and cold."

The neighbors in Farmington, Maine, had always been impressed by Chester's drive and initiative. As one of six kids in a farm family on the back Falls Road struggling to make ends meet, Chester did his best to help out. The family kept several laying hens, and Chester walked an eight-mile route from house to house selling eggs. Sometimes he sold fudge or other candies such as peppermints and drop sweets that he himself had made.

But for all Chester's industry, the flash of inspiration for his famous kid invention came to him at a moment when he had decided to relax and have some fun.

One day in the winter of 1873, Chester walked to nearby Abbot Pond to try out a pair of new skates. The nip in the air sent him racing home. He found "Gram" in the farmhouse kitchen and asked her to help him fashion something to shield his ears. Chester's ears itched fiercely at the touch of wool, so the everyday muffler most kids wrapped about their heads was out of the question.

The Greenwood Champion Ear Protector, as he later called the device, didn't take much time to put together. Chester supplied the idea and the material; his grandmother's fingers contributed the sewing skill. It was breathtakingly simple. The muff required bending some wire, cutting soft insulating material, and then sewing a few stitches.

To shield his ears, Chester decided on a combination of beaver fur on the outside and black velvet for the surface against the ear. For the headband, he chose a soft wire known as farm wire, a precursor of baling wire. Some accounts say the contraption was then attached to his cap.

The Ear Protector proved an instant hit. All over Farmington and in the surrounding community, kids started to pester their parents and grandparents to make the thing.

Despite his friends' enthusiasm, Chester wasn't satisfied. The first model didn't work so well. "The ears flapped too much," according to his granddaughter Jackie. Like many inventions, the Greenwood earmuff was a great idea that needed some refinements.

The first step was a change in materials. Chester decided to try flat spring steel, three-eighths of an inch wide, for the band. Two improvements resulted: the new band enabled him to attach a tiny hinge to each ear flap so the muff

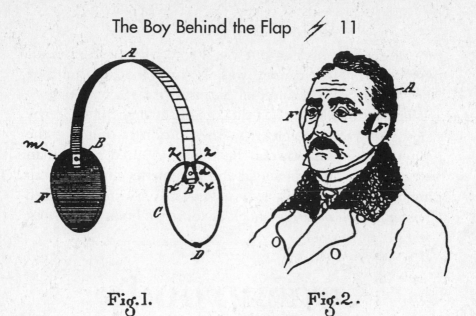

Fig.1.    Fig.2.

*From Chester Greenwood's patent for "new
and useful Improvements in Ear-Mufflers"*

could fit snugly against his ears. And the springy steel allowed him, when he was finished using the muff, to coil it
flat and stuff the contraption in his pocket.

The result? Greenwood had an invention that took on a
life of its own. Everyone, not just kids or people allergic to
wool, had to have the Ear Protector.

In the beginning, the popular muff sold in one style. "Like
Henry Ford's auto, the Ear Protector came in any color
you wanted as long as it was black," says grandson George.
Chester seemed pretty satisfied with it. "I believe perfec-
tion has been reached," he stated in advertising his earmuff.

On March 13, 1877, the United States Patent Office
awarded him patent #188,292. Greenwood was just eighteen years old at the time. Soon after, he established a factory in a brick building in West Farmington, a place he
called The Shop. Later, Chester expanded to Front Street
in downtown Farmington and had more than twenty full-

time employees turning out Ear Protectors on the second floor. In 1883, his factory was producing 30,000 muffs a year, and by 1936 the annual output had risen to 400,000.

When he died in 1937 at the age of seventy-nine, Greenwood was a Maine celebrity. In addition to running the muff business, Greenwood had been granted more than 130 patents. They included improvements on the spark plug, a decoy mouse trap called the Mechanical Cat, Chester's version of the shock absorber, a hook for pulling

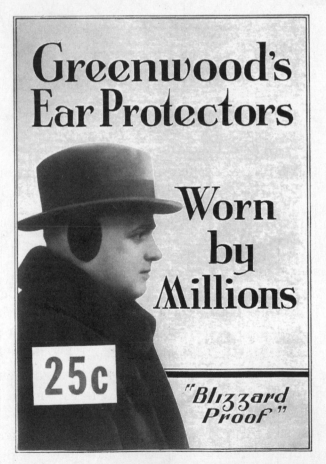

*Advertisement with Chester Greenwood's son Clinton as a model*

doughnuts from boiling oil, the Rubberless Rubber Band, and the Greenwood Tempered Steel Rake ("Use me right and I'll serve you for years," proclaimed the label).

Curiously, even after Greenwood automated most of The Shop, his muff business couldn't do without hands that could sew. There was only one way to attach fabric to the hinged flap, the way Gram had done it in the farm kitchen when they made the first model. Women and men in the area took the piecework home, and it spread as a cottage industry, an industry whose labor force is made up of people working at home. Chester's kid invention, in its heyday, "supported half of Franklin County," according to one resident.

# VANESSA HESS
## A COLORFUL IDEA

On the first Friday in January 1991, Vanessa Hess sat in her seventh-grade science classroom at Stonybrook Junior High and heard her teacher, Mrs. Maurine Marchani, announce that each kid had to do a new project—they had to invent something.

"There are only two ways you can avoid this," Mrs. Marchani said. "You can die, or you can move."

As Mrs. Marchani continued, she made it clear that this was *not* a science-fair type of project. "I never want to see another papier-mâché volcano," she said.

Mrs. Marchani wanted to see original inventions. There must be any number of schools across the United States where science teachers encourage students to be creative by saying, "Maybe someday you'll grow up to be a famous inventor." To Vanessa's dismay, Mrs. Marchani had different advice. Why not try to become a famous inventor *right now?*

In the Indianapolis area, Maurine Marchani has made a name for herself by inspiring her kids to become inventors. One of her students, Steve Prater, has been featured in national magazines. Twice, he won prizes in competitions for his inventions. One invention was something called a Hand

Stabilizer, a device that enabled a friend of his with cerebral palsy to hold a pencil and write responses on true-false or multiple-choice tests. It worked so well he patented the Hand Stabilizer and began developing it commercially. In his honor, the mayor of Indianapolis proclaimed August 23, 1989, Steve Prater Day.

"But me?" Vanessa asked herself. Once, Mrs. Marchani had instructed her students to figure out ways to drop an egg from the school roof without the egg breaking as it landed. When the teacher, dressed in a bunny suit, tried Vanessa's idea, the results weren't so great. "Mine crushed," says Vanessa.

In spite of her doubts, however, this hesitant inventor had her idea after only a few weeks. In the classroom, Mrs. Marchani had said that when inventors hit upon a great idea, they sometimes shout a loud and victorious "Ah-hah!" But Vanessa? Her idea came as a soft "Hmmm . . ."

It all started on the last weekend in January, when spring-like weather visited Indianapolis. The warm sunny day found Vanessa and her dad in the driveway, washing and waxing the family car.

The maroon Olds gleamed as if new. But Vanessa noticed that each scratch in the paint showed up as a white mark, the white being wax left in the scratch.

"You ought to cover these scratches," she said.

"Don't know how to," her father replied. "Unless I go to an auto-parts store and get some touch-up paint. And even then, it may not match."

"There ought to be a wax with color in it."

"There isn't one."

"Why not?"

"I don't know."

And she had her idea. She stored it away inside her head and kept hoping a better one would come along. For a while, she thought of developing something to keep apples from turning brown after paring. But every Friday afternoon when Mrs. Marchani checked on her students' progress, Vanessa shrugged and didn't say much.

As the February due date drew near, Vanessa realized she was running out of time. A few calls to auto-supply stores and a quick check through an auto magazine indicated that no one else seemed to have produced a colored car wax. So far, so good. Vanessa bought a blue Matchbox car and added blue food coloring to some car wax. She scratched up the toy car, then waxed the thing—and it worked!

That Thursday night, with some encouragement from her mother, Vanessa printed up a posterboard and readied her display. "It wasn't real nice," she admits, "just a quick job." The next day in the classroom she stared uneasily at more attractive presentations. But Mrs. Marchani, moving from student to student, had an eye for true ingenuity. When she poked her face over Vanessa's shoulder, she stared at the display for a moment, taking it in. Then in a level tone she prophesied, "You are going to make money from this."

Vanessa's colored car wax won first place in her classroom, and then swept the field in a competition against inventions from other classes at Stonybrook. A panel of judges picked Vanessa's project to represent Stonybrook in the annual contest sponsored by Invent America!, a national organization that works with schools to encourage young people to invent. Her display won that summer at the state level.

That October, a newspaper article about Vanessa resulted in a phone call to the Hess home. An auto-products company had already been developing colored car wax with an industrial chemist—by coincidence, it was an Indianapolis firm.

The annals of invention are strewn with bitter disputes between inventors claiming the same product. But this story has a happy ending: the owners of the auto-products company, two brothers named Dan and Don Huffman, were charmed by Vanessa's story and decided to ask her to appear in an "infomercial" for Magic Shine, their colored car wax. Contracts were signed, and Vanessa and her mom were well paid to fly to California to help make a Magic Shine promotional movie that was later broadcast on television all over the country.

How did the young inventor like moviemaking? Vanessa ponders the days in Hollywood rehearsing and shooting and taking instructions from the British director. "It was kinda nice," is all she says.

The success of Vanessa Hess also belongs to her teacher. Maurine Marchani seems to provide classroom experiences that lead to creative thinking. In fact, entering Mrs. Marchani's classroom is itself an experience. Visitors must find their way past a whole zoo of floppy sculptures that dangle from the wall. A live rabbit hops up and down the rows between the desks. A rabbit? "If you don't pet her," says Mrs. Marchani, "she eats your shoelaces."

The science teacher has a theory that junior-high-school kids need more physical attention than they admit. A kid who enters the school from a stressed-out home may need to have a rabbit on his lap the whole period.

And she also believes that this is just the kind of place that encourages kids to risk having original thoughts. "In a setting that's offbeat, it's O.K. to make a mistake," says Mrs. Marchani. "Kids are afraid of being foolish. If the teacher is sort of silly, then it's O.K. for them. It's O.K. to risk."

She also notes that the students with the highest grade-point averages aren't always the best inventors. "I find that kids who do not do well on paper-and-pencil tests do wonderful things with ideas."

Some people view kid inventions as flukes. But Maurine Marchani disagrees. "Nobody's told seventh-graders they aren't creative yet," she says. To her mind, when it comes to inventing, twelve is the perfect age.

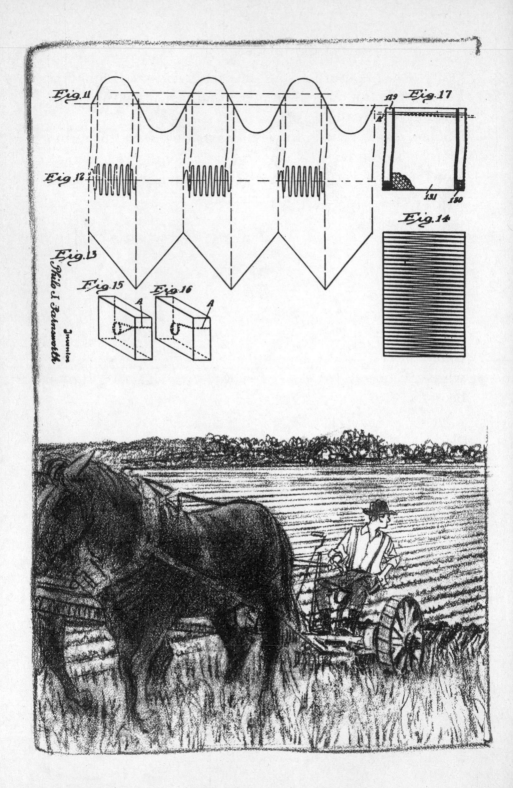

Fig. 11

Fig. 17

119

B

Fig. 12

Fig. 14

131    130

Fig. 13

Fig. 15    Fig. 16

A    A

Invention

Philo J. Farnsworth

# PHILO T. FARNSWORTH
## PLOWBOY INVENTOR

In the spring of 1921, a fourteen-year-old farm boy came up with the idea for television as we know it today. His name was Philo T. Farnsworth and the place where he was hit by the spark of invention was a sugar-beet field on the family farm near Rigby, Idaho.

Young Philo had been driving a disc harrow, a machine pulled by two horses that crumbled and smoothed the soil. Although the work was drudgery, the job gave him time to think.

In 1921, the Age of Radio had barely dawned (there were fewer than thirty licensed radio stations in the country), but people were looking to the future: if sound could be sent through the air, why not pictures, too?

This question had been under investigation for many years. In 1884, Paul Nipkow received a German patent for a method of television transmission which depended on light from a scene passing through holes in a spinning disk to a light-sensitive photocell in order to break an image down into an electrical signal. Since then, many improved systems had been developed, all mechanical. Some of the great scientists of the day, such as C. F. Jenkins in Washington, D.C., and John L. Baird in Scotland, were working on the problem. So was Philo T. Farnsworth.

Philo was an avid reader of popular-science magazines. Inspired by articles in their pages, he had been trying for more than a year to figure out how to create television. As his future wife later wrote, "Bit by bit he collected information that eventually led him to discover [for himself] that mysterious, vitally important particle called the electron, the study of which would define his life . . . Philo tried to imagine a way to use electrons to eliminate the mechanical method of transmitting pictures." The solution first came to him when he looked back over his shoulder in the sugar-beet field. He saw the neat rows his harrow had just made in the earth. The pattern gave him an idea for using electrons in similar rows to make the television picture.

Philo knew that other inventors' elaborate and clunky mechanical systems for turning images into electrical signals, some of them hand cranked, would never work fast enough. To transmit a clear picture, he figured the complete image would have to be completely "scanned" or broken down many times per second, much faster than the spinning disks could be rotated. The other inventors were all "barking up the wrong tree," said Philo.

He was born in 1906 in a log cabin. His father and mother were the children of Mormon pioneers who had trekked

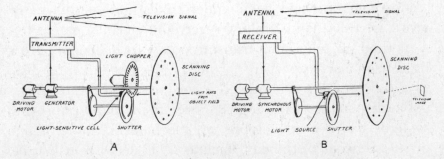

*John L. Baird's mechanical television system*

across the deserts to establish a promised land in the West, and had endured some difficult times. Like many other farm families, they depended on income from good crop prices to keep up with mortgage payments on their property. More than once, crop prices dropped so low that they lost their home. When this happened, the family would migrate to the next farm or ranch across the sagebrush flats.

The Farnsworth children worked hard. One job the children shared was thinning the sugar beets. Sugar beets are planted in long, orderly rows and the kids needed to move down the rows, removing extra seedlings with a slice of the hoe so that the remaining plants would have plenty of space to grow.

"The rows seemed forever," remembers his younger sister Agnes. As they worked in the field, Philo talked with his brothers and sisters about a scheme for electronic television. He felt he could make money from this idea, and Agnes, who looked up to her dreamy older brother, thought this development "was just around the corner."

Whatever would come next, Philo knew he didn't want to farm. "I had decided before I was twelve that I could be an inventor," he remembered later when testifying before patent examiners.

In 1919, he scored his first success. Hugo Gernsback's *Science and Invention* magazine sponsored a contest, promising a $25 prize to the amateur who came up with the most valuable invention to enhance the comfort of the automobile. Philo submitted an idea for a magnetized ignition and key to deter thieves.

His ingenious design won the prize and the local paper trumpeted the news. However, beyond his hometown and a few relatives, no one knew that the winner of this national contest was a thirteen-year-old kid.

Philo's original plan had been to spend his prize money on scientific books, but by September, when the check arrived in the mail, the Farnsworths were low on cash. The money went for school clothes instead, including Philo's first pair of long pants.

In September 1921, as a freshman at the high school in Rigby, Idaho, he was enrolled in the freshman science course. But before long he showed up in the doorway of the principal's office with a special request.

Philo asked permission to enter the senior chemistry class. Impossible, replied the principal. So Philo sought out the teacher, Justin Tolman. Tolman turned Philo down, too, although he lent him some science books from his personal library. But Tolman hadn't heard the last of Philo's request. When midterm arrived, the freshman marched back into Tolman's office. He wanted to sign up for the second half of senior chemistry. A few questions satisfied the teacher that Philo had learned much from his reading. But, Tolman asked, how could he expect to keep up with senior boys, who had completed three months of difficult work?

Philo left, and Tolman thought the matter at an end, until the next afternoon, when Philo appeared before him again. Could he just sit in with the senior boys? Impressed by his determination, Tolman finally agreed and offered to tutor Philo so he could catch up.

"I had known hundreds of boys," Tolman later said, as a witness before the Patent Office in defense of Philo's patent claims. "But he was the one I knew was different."

Tolman at first didn't know how different. One afternoon when he arrived at the empty classroom where he tutored Philo, he found a surprise. The boy stood at the blackboard, having covered almost every inch with elaborate electrical circuit diagrams and equations neatly lined and printed. Philo then confessed the reason behind his intense scientific study. He had conceived of an electronic television system, all of his own design, and he needed the know-how to make his scheme work.

Could Tolman look his diagrams over and offer helpful criticism? Did the idea even make sense? Tolman went through the diagrams step by step, asking questions. To every objection, Philo had an answer, or at least he felt reasonably confident that snarls could be worked out.

Philo explained that his system would "use the electron to take the moving parts out of television." At the heart of Philo's plan was what he conceived in the sugar-beet field. He named this basic part the Image Dissector and around it Philo built his television camera.

The Image Dissector consisted of a vacuum tube that would convert images into usable electronic information. The image to be sent would be focused by a lens onto a photoelectric surface inside the vacuum tube. Researchers had long known that photoelectrically sensitive surfaces change light into electrical impulses of varying intensities, but two problems stopped them from using this to make a television camera. First, the electrons did not emit from the photoelectric surface in straight, parallel lines. Second, the

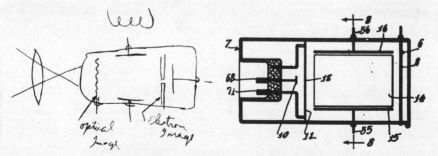

*Philo Farnsworth's 1922 notebook sketch of the Image Dissector, drawn for Justin Tolman, and the refinement for a patent filed five years later. (Drawings are oriented in opposite directions)*

electrons flew off the photoelectric surface with widely varying velocities. What was the result? Instead of variations in the electron flow neatly copying variations in the light flow, the electrons danced in a wild jumble.

Philo had a clever solution to this problem. Remembering a research article that said a magnetic field could guide an electron beam, he came up with the brainstorm of wrapping electronic coils around the tube. The coils created a magnetic field inside the tube that would guide the electrons in lines as orderly as the rows in a field.

On the receiving end, Philo reversed the effect. Inside another vacuum tube, electronic information was turned into visual information glowing on a photosensitive screen. Philo proposed to guide the electrons in this cathode-ray (electron beam) picture tube by means of a magnetic field, so they lay down in neat lines to duplicate the picture on the transmitting end.

The biggest obstacle Justin Tolman foresaw was patents. And Philo knew this, too. The Patent Office no longer required the inventor to submit a working model, but "operativeness" was still a key issue. Would the contraption work? That was the question—not only for the patent examiner but for any investors Philo hoped to persuade to give him backing. He needed to start a pilot project, and he didn't have the money.

In the spring of 1922, Philo had to quit school early. The family needed him in the fields, and he never returned to Rigby High. That summer, he completed a correspondence course to earn an electrician's license, and found a job with a railroad in Idaho. In the fall, the family moved to Provo, and Philo joined them a year later. He enrolled as a special student at Brigham Young University in order to earn enough credits to finish his high-school education.

In Provo, Philo continued his inventive thinking, with his father's blessing. Philo's father had faith in his son's ideas, even though he didn't understand them. He encouraged Philo to try to patent a simple idea that could be immediately developed and sold. Using the quick earnings for "seed money," Philo could then begin work on his television system.

Philo had many inventions in mind. One, a discovery he scrawled on a notebook page, was a nifty scheme for a fine-tuning radio dial that would bring better reception. Philo and his father answered the ad of a mail-order patent-attorney service. They sent the design and $200 in savings to the Washington, D.C., company. They received no reply and to their knowledge nothing came of it.

Later, however, Philo read that someone else had patented the radio dial. He saw that his original drawing fit the product design exactly and believed his idea had been stolen. But the Farnsworths didn't have the money to fight a legal battle.

If patent pirates would so quickly grab a mere gadget, how much more dangerous would it be to stake out a claim in something as huge and promising as television?

In January 1924, Philo's father died. In the months that followed, all the children were forced to find work. Philo slipped through a series of jobs as janitor, lumberjack, radio repairman, and door-to-door salesman. He even joined the navy, although he was soon honorably released at his mother's request, since he was the main breadwinner for the family.

In the fall, Philo began his freshman year at Brigham Young University in Provo, Utah. His professors were fascinated by this peculiar student—but not by his idea for television, which they thought unworkable.

Then Philo's luck took a turn for the better.

In the spring of 1926, he found a job as a temporary office worker in Salt Lake City. His employers were two men from San Francisco, George Everson and Leslie Gorrell, who had come to town to establish a local Community Chest, a charitable organization.

One evening when the workers were completing a late mailing, Everson asked Philo about his plans for the future. At first the young clerk shrugged off the question. Everson later wrote in his biography that Farnsworth "looked much older than his nineteen years." He also recalled "a nervous tension about him that was probably the result of financial worry."

Then Philo decided to reveal to Everson and Gorrell his dream of television. "As the discussion started," Everson said, "Farnsworth's personality seemed to change. His eyes, always pleasant, began burning with eagerness and conviction; his speech, which usually was halting, became fluent to the point of eloquence as he described . . . this scheme that had occupied his mind for the last four years."

Their talks continued over the next week whenever the workers found free time. Everson was a conservative businessman and had no technical background. Although Gorrell knew little about experimental electronics, he held a degree in civil engineering and could grasp the basics of Philo's plans. Eventually, Everson decided to risk $6,000 in savings in support of Philo's scheme. The three would be partners, and Gorrell would reimburse Everson half the money, if the investment turned sour.

What convinced him, Everson said, "was faith in the ability of the boy inventor."

In a short time, Everson and Gorrell decided Philo should relocate to California, where he could take advantage of advice from skilled technical workers who had established themselves near the California Institute of Technology, and have easy access to specialty items available in scientific and industrial supply shops in the Bay Area. Soon after the move, Philo and his backers realized they needed more money. After trying elsewhere, Everson arranged an interview with a personal friend at the Crocker First National Bank of San Francisco. However, the day Everson and Philo arrived, they discovered Everson's friend was not there, and they found themselves being ushered into the office of James J. Fagan.

Fagan was a legend on the West Coast. His clients said he could smell a bad investment walking through the door. Philo had to stand up before this stranger and explain his idea. When he finished, Fagan said the scheme was a "damn fool" idea. Then he grinned and added, "But somebody ought to put money into it."

Crocker Bank arranged for a group of investors to back them with $25,000, more than Philo and his partners had dared to ask for. Later, as the papers were being drawn up, there was a glitch. Philo explained that he would need to send them back to Utah to get his mother's signature. He was, after all, only nineteen years old and (in 1926) legally still a minor.

In the fall of that year, Philo started operating his own experimental lab at 202 Green Street in San Francisco. Freed of immediate financial worry and able to get his hands on state-of-the-art equipment and supplies, he moved quickly. Also, he had the help of his new bride, Elma, whom he called "Pem." He and Pem had fallen in love as students at Brigham Young. Soon after the wedding, Pem Farnsworth found herself not only managing the lab office but also doing Philo's technical drawings and helping out with spot-welding. Philo also hired Cliff, Pem's brother and his best friend from Provo, with whom he used to build and sell crystal radio sets. Cliff, like Philo, was a sagebrush farm boy with no special training in experimental electronics, but with a lot of sweat and hard work, he soon learned the advanced glassblowing skills needed to create vacuum tubes.

Philo and his small staff raced to complete a working model. Would some other team unknown to them beat

Philo to production with the same idea? Would his own financial backers grow restless if there were no quick returns, and decide to sell the project to a large corporation which then might replace Philo with its in-house staff? Many worries hounded the young inventor.

When he built his television, Philo was starting from scratch—he had to invent the basic components to put together his invention. Philo and his helpers had to wind their own electrical coils, setting down one layer at a time, shellacking the copper wire firmly into place. They built cathode tubes and amplifiers the world had never seen. He devised a shielded grid in his Image Dissector to keep stray electrons from interfering with the ones that would make his picture.

On September 7, 1927, Philo made television history when he transmitted the first all-electronic television picture. A line appeared on the screen of his receiver in the Green Street lab. When the slide from which the image was being scanned was turned ninety degrees, the line on the receiver did the same. Soon after his twenty-first birthday, the young inventor had proved his scheme would work.

Eight months later, the first two-dimensional images were broadcast: a triangle, and then, for the benefit of the investors, a dollar sign. During one of the demonstrations, Cliff blew smoke into the transmitter from a cigarette, and the cloud became the first moving television image to appear on the receiver's screen.

What remains of Philo T. Farnsworth's story involves his achievements as an adult. As George Everson put it, "It actually took more than $1,000,000 in money and thirteen years in time before his invention was ready for commercialization."

In the years that followed, Philo achieved success as the head of research for Farnsworth Television, Inc. But tele-

*Philo Farnsworth in 1929 at the controls of his company's first manufactured television set. The white circle is the screen and to the right is the speaker*

vision turned out to be not one invention but really a network of inventions, all interlaced, and many companies and inventors contributed to its development. Although competition from huge companies, especially the Radio Corporation of America (RCA), took its toll in stress and financial ups and downs for him, Philo always battled on. When companies challenged Farnsworth Television claims with interference suits at the Patent Office, Philo always won his case.

In the end, more than a thousand patents were required to perfect television. Of these, Philo originated more than 160 and shared in hundreds of others, many of them crucial advances. And at the root of it all was the idea that he first thought of as a boy in an Idaho field.

# JERRALD SPENCER
## THE DAZZLER

Eureka! *Voilà!* Ah-hah! I got it! Bingo! Most stories of invention have a magic moment of inspiration. For Jerrald Spencer, the moment came when he was fifteen years old.

It was a December night in 1977, and a series of experiments in Jerrald's basement had failed. "It was a pretty farfetched idea," the inventor admits, "but I was trying to fly magnetically." Sometime after midnight, the discouraged young man gave up. Staring at his reflection in the dim basement bathroom mirror, he waved a lit cigarette back and forth, tracing patterns against the darkness.

And then it happened.

What he saw in the mirror inspired his first marketed invention. The invention was to become Light Show, a device resulting in a whole galaxy of sparkling toys that have sold more than five million units.

Magnetism and electricity had long been Jerrald Spencer's favorite subjects, and much of what he knew was self-taught. He took a hands-on approach to learning, and this approach—when he was thirteen and interested in chemistry—almost took his hands *off*. He blew up the family garage. "I'm still wearing the scars today," he says.

After the chemical explosion, he decided to study electronics. For Jerrald, studying meant taking things apart, things such as the family's appliances, radios, tape players, and televisions. Out of desperation, his mother, Carolyn, began to search secondhand shops in the St. Louis area to buy him broken electrical appliances to use instead. Fortunately, he didn't fry himself on the high voltages stored on the rear surface of TV picture tubes long after the set is turned off. "I just needed to learn a few things," explains Jerrald today.

He set up a workshop in the basement, where he began using discards from the world of consumer electronics to put together all sorts of strange new devices. According to Jerrald, "My friends were always wondering: 'What's he got cooking?' I didn't know at the time I was inventing. I was just building what I wanted to have and it wasn't available on the market."

The Spencers didn't have an easy life. They were a single-parent family with six kids (Jerrald was the second). Carolyn worked two jobs as a medical lab assistant to make ends meet, and the family often moved as she struggled to find a better neighborhood. Jerrald went from one school system to the next, with the result that classroom education never quite "clicked" for this obviously gifted teenager. And his long, exhilarating bouts of experimentation into the wee hours of the morning didn't help him keep awake the next day at his desk.

In the seventh grade, Jerrald was kicked out of school, apparently because a science teacher felt he had tried to upstage a tuning-fork demonstration. Despite this, Jerrald remained confident. "Mom, don't worry," he said again and again, and on his own he completed a GED, the high-school equivalency certificate, and continued to invent.

Carolyn proudly remembers the inventions he created, the robots that he commanded to hold tea cups and to march down stairs; the go-carts assembled from lawn-mower motors and Big Wheels that zipped over long distances. And then there was what became known as Light Show—the device that led to professional success.

What was this gizmo? It certainly didn't resemble a boy with a cigarette. In his final version, Jerrald had soldered together several circuit boards that had glowing display lights, taken from old stereos, and he rotated them on motors salvaged from broken tape recorders. The thing had two rotations: one small, one large, each at different speeds—just as the cigarette in his hand spun in one circle at his wrist while his arm flung around in a broader one. The result, reasoned Jerrald, was a pattern resembling an electron rotating while following its orbit around the nucleus of an atom.

In broad daylight, it didn't look great. But in the dark it was something exciting and different, a captivating eruption of light patterns.

In the early days he called his device the Atomic Simulator. He seriously meant to duplicate the pattern of an electron as it races around the nucleus of an atom. "I wanted to make a large atom," he says—a macro-version of the minute particles that shape our world.

In an encyclopedia, under an article about quartz, Jerrald discovered the same patterns, the same procession of shapes he witnessed at night in his basement, in diagrams showing the symmetry of quartz crystals. He describes having the sense that what he invented was simply something recalled from another existence.

"I knew I was dealing with powers that we are not familiar with," says Jerrald, "the same forces that keep the planets in line and keep us glued to the earth."

He found himself dropping to his knees and praying for safety every evening before beginning another round of experiments with these eerie, primal patterns of light.

Today Jerrald laughs at some of his farfetched notions. But he still takes the Simulator, which he now calls the Hologram Generator, seriously. In his mind, as a fifteen-year-old high-school dropout, he really did drop in on the basic forces in our world. Jerrald is convinced his device can record magnetic fields and aura patterns around the human body, and that recordings made when one is healthy can be compared to those made when one is ill, to aid diagnosis.

But how to make money? When he was twenty years old,

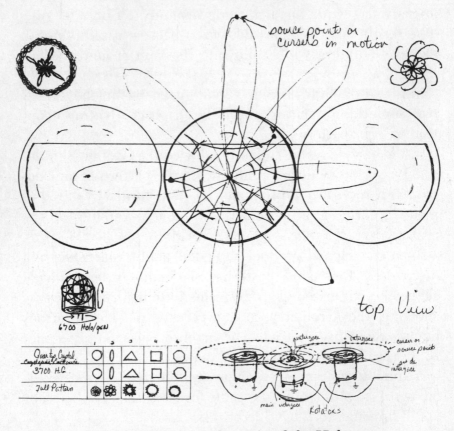

*Jerrald Spencer's schematic of the Hologram Generator*

Jerrald had to find a good way to support his wife and new-born child. He had dreamed of making money from the medical uses which he envisioned for the Hologram Generator. But he knew from the stringent government regulations on medical research that he didn't have a chance in that field.

Instead, he showed his invention to a businessman, Bev Taylor, who owned a toy company named Steven Manufacturing. Taylor was dazzled. His associates at Steven Manufacturing liked the young inventor, too. "Jerrald's an absolute boilermaker," says Jim McNulty, a St. Louis retail specialist who first saw the Generator and introduced Jerrald to Taylor. "Ideas come out of him all the time—an unbelievable creative genius."

In 1988, the company started a whole series of Light Show toys, each containing a simplified version of Jerrald's original device. Since then, more than five million sparkling toys have been sold, and the most popular, the Lightning Bug Push Toy, can be found on the shelves of Wal-Mart, Kmart, and other retailers nationwide.

Today Steven Manufacturing ranks as a leading company in its specialty field. When the company was sold recently, the new owners paid Jerrald a retainer fee to stay and dream up new toys. Jerrald Spencer has created lots of fun for millions of kids. Who knows what's next? By his estimate, some one hundred inventions from his teenage basement experiments remain untested—and he has new ideas all the time.

# CATHY EVANS
## A MATERIAL SUCCESS

**O**ne Sunday afternoon when she was twelve years old, Cathy Evans opened the door of an empty room at her cousin's farmhouse, where she was visiting. The room was dimly lit and smelled of dust and stale air. But Cathy hardly noticed. Her attention was drawn to a spread draped on the bed, a coverlet with beautiful patterns formed by curious small tufts, an heirloom that had been handed down for generations. It was a moment that would change the course of the farm girl's life. It would change thirty thousand other lives, too, for that is roughly how many people later came to earn their wages in the tufted-bedspread industry.

Fascinated with her discovery, Cathy started pestering her aunt and mother with questions. Who had made the fabulous spread? How did she do it? Where were these wonders produced? No one knew for sure. It had been brought to the mountains of northern Georgia by some colonial family. For Cathy, one thing was certain. "When I grow older, I'm going to make me one," she said.

Born August 10, 1880, the second of six children, Cathy grew up on a red-clay farm outside Dalton, Georgia. She saw the bedspread in the summer of 1892. For some time after, without any urgency, she played with ideas of how to make a spread of her own—there were no deadlines, no schedules, just a "fancy" moving her. As a Southern farm girl, she lived in a world of cotton—so cotton would have to be her raw material. Not having yarn thick enough, she took two candlewicks (each made from six strands, or plies) and ran them off on the spinning wheel to make a twelve-ply yarn. Because she lacked wooden spools, she wound the homemade yarn on corncobs. Recent evidence suggests that the backing for her first spread was old cotton sacks sewn together. Without any pattern to use as a guide, she used quilting frames to mark the surface of the spread with a grid of three-inch squares to structure the vast labor before her. Without an artist to help, she found an old quilt design and copied it. And when she had barely reached her fifteenth birthday, she started a spread.

"You started something you will never finish," said her mother. But during what she called her "recreation hours" Cathy worked, unwrapping her project on the dinner table or sometimes the bedroom floor, and many months later she did finish. The result drew praise from family and friends. It was so much labor, however, that she vowed never to do it again. Then, according to Cathy, "one year later, I had forgotten the trouble and enjoyed [having the spread] so much that in 1896 I decided to make another one."

Cathy had brought to life a craft that may have originated with pioneer housewives in the American colonies. When they mended holes in old spreads, the colonial ladies fluffed the thread ends at the darned place into decorative balls and added other balls to create a design.

Cathy, however, arrived independently at her own working process, and her methods were ingenious. For her backings, she began using unbleached cotton sheetings sewn together. Her basic tool was a four-inch bodkin needle, a big, queer-looking needle, curved on one end, that was designed for pushing materials as large as ribbon through a fabric. Using her candlewick yarn, she made large single stitches linking equidistant dots marked along the line of her design, at each dot drawing the yarn down through the fabric and up again. Then she clipped the stitches in the center between the dots, leaving two ends of yarn protruding from each dot. By laundering the finished spread, Cathy untwisted and fluffed the twenty-four plies of the two ends of yarn. The result was a tuft, a ball of tangled threads.

She laundered and relaundered and then hung the spread to bleach in the sun, a process that removed the stains and pencil markings and tightened the hold of the yarn to the base through shrinkage. One worker later recalled, "You would brush them while they were damp and that would fluff the stitch up." Finally, Cathy hung the spread on a clothesline and let the mountain winds blow her handiwork to ensure that the tufts would be as fluffy as possible.

At nineteen, Cathy took a spread to Trion, Georgia, as a wedding gift for her brother and his bride. The guests showered Cathy with praise for her work. A lady wanted to buy one. "Mrs. Lange told me to make it, and whatever I said it was worth would be all right with her," Cathy later recalled. The shy farm girl could hardly believe that her homemade product had value. She set her price at $2.50, leaving pitifully little after expenses. "She wanted to pay more, but I did not want to charge too much. Back then, a man worked for a dollar a day."

The bedspread that Cathy made for Mrs. Lange was the first of many she made to order. Her spread was a useful item—and lovely. Orders for spreads began to come through the mail to the Evans farmhouse, and when the trickle became a stream, it was obvious that she had invented a marketable product.

Right from the start, Cathy thought up new ideas to streamline the work. She later explained one of her improvements:

*I put a worked [finished] spread on the floor [face side up], put the spread to be stamped over it, and by rubbing with a tin box lid—which had been rubbed on a meat skin—made the pattern to be worked appear in black dots [in other words, grease from the skin acted like a crayon and washed off later]. This made it much easier to do. I filled my orders right along.*

Cathy came up with other refinements. Although her first patterns seem to have been copied from old quilts, she later created her own designs and gave them names—Wild Rose, Star and Circle, Acorn, Flower Basket, Square Circle, and many others. Her earliest spreads were white, but when she located a factory in Rhode Island which would dye her yarns with color that didn't run in laundering, she was able to make multicolored bedspreads, too.

As demand increased, Cathy had so much to do she needed help from her friends. According to a local resident: "She taught her neighbors, and her neighbors taught their neighbors, and before you knew it, all kinds of people were working."

The road that meandered past the Evans farm was typical of thousands of roads in northern Georgia, a dirt byway connecting small farms whose residents tried to wrest a living from the stubborn clay. There was no electricity, few automobiles, and sometimes not even a mule. But by 1912 these Georgians suddenly found themselves overwhelmed with orders from distant cities for something they could make by hand on their own time.

To some, Cathy's invention became known as "turfing," because the tufts looked like clumps of grass turf. But the popular name was "tufting," and it was the magical word in the air. Witnesses from those years remember driving

*Cathy Evans, in later life, with one of her tufted spreads*

down country roads and at every farm seeing not just the women and girls but the men and boys, too, "tufting" on the front porch. The production of spreads had become a rewarding cottage industry.

Along U.S. Highway 41 in the area, nearly every farmhouse offered tufted bedspreads for sale, the colorful products flapping from clotheslines. That stretch of road became nationally famous as Bedspread Boulevard.

Millions of dollars poured into the Georgia economy as a result of sales not just to motorists passing through but to retail stores across the country, including Marshall Field's in Chicago. Cathy's competitors demonstrated their inventiveness, too, thinking up new methods, new stitches, and creating new designs. In the 1930s, tufting machines were invented (by a former Edison assistant who came to town), and Dalton factories began mass-producing the spreads.

Cathy never developed her own business into a big company, perhaps because she didn't have the funds for major investments, but she was proud of what she had started. She said the spreads had been "bread and butter in the day of scarcity."

Later the spread fashion faded, the cotton yarns and fabrics needed began to disappear with the advent of acrylics and polyester in the late 1950s, and the Georgia tufting companies decided greater profits lay in carpeting. When it was discovered that a backing of jute fiber could be used to anchor synthetic yarn, tufting replaced weaving as the process of choice for carpet makers. Today, more than ninety percent of the carpets we walk on are tufted, a development that can be traced back to Cathy.

Several years before her death in 1964, Cathy Evans Whitener appeared at a local school. In a speech to the students, she said:

*When I was a girl I wished that I had been a boy. Because a boy could find work to make money, and there was nothing a girl could do to earn money. I feel now that God knew best, and I am glad I was a girl.*

# Frank W. Epperson
## SWEETNESS ON A STICK

There it was. The boy held the concoction in his hand: a glass containing flavored soda water left outside overnight. It had frozen. All over San Francisco, a cold snap had worked its magic and even the surface of Stow Lake in Golden Gate Park had turned solid. His mixing stick was frozen into the mixture, too, and now protruded like a handle. But the warmth from the palm of his hand was enough: the icy mass slipped free of the glass and his fingers clutched the wooden stick. The year was 1905. At age eleven, Frank W. Epperson was holding the world's first Popsicle.

Later, Frank's story became a tall tale embellished by newspaper writers who claimed he had accidentally left the mixture on the back porch, had forgotten to remove his stirring rod, and been blessed by a once-in-a-decade cold spell.

But the real story is different. What was he doing the night of the big freeze?

"Experimenting," said Frank, when he recollected events later for a memoir handed down in his family.

As he walked to school that morning, he carried the thing in his hand. His friends crowded around for a taste, delighted with his discovery. Frank hadn't yet coined a name. "Fruit icicle" . . . "frozen treat on a stick" . . . "Ep-sicle" . . . various names eventually came to mind, and it would be years before the name Popsicle was chosen. All Frank knew at this point was that he "had a pretty pink frozen lollypop."

Frank W. Epperson was born on August 11, 1894, at Willows, California, and grew up in the San Francisco Bay area. His father, Henry, had dreamed up several inventions and one of these, Epperson's Patented Kiln, was used in the family business, a chinaware company.

As a child, Frank worked for his father after school in the shop. He learned a machinist's skills by running the equipment that produced the ceramics. In addition, he developed an artistic bent, because the Eppersons hand-painted the china they sold.

But how did an eleven-year-old boy think up the Popsicle? It started in his neighborhood. The kids had decided to build a mini-amusement park on the lawn across the street from the Epperson home, and Frank was assigned to run the soda-water stand. Even before this, however, he had been experimenting. He would buy packets of soda powder and flavors at the grocery store and try to mix exotic drinks. Perhaps Frank had in mind the case of a Georgia pharmacist who in 1886 substituted soda water for flat tap water in his "health drink" and found that people began to consume the stuff for fun. The drink was Coca-Cola.

Whatever his inspiration, Frank was ready when the mercury fell in the thermometers. "I wondered how [the snack] would taste frozen so I left a little in a glass overnight on the back porch," wrote the inventor in his unpublished memoir.

Happy with the first results, Frank tried repeatedly to

duplicate them, but that winter Bay Area temperatures never dropped so low again. And although ice-making plants were fairly widespread at the time (to keep up with the demand created by the home ice chest) the home electric freezer was still decades away. Frank did not have the money to invest in large-scale industrial freezing machines, and he could not rely on freakishly cold winter weather in California to create what was essentially a summer delight.

For several years, Frank kept the development of his frozen treat on hold. After the 1919 Armistice that ended the First World War, he went to work in the real-estate business in Oakland, California. By that time, he was married, the father of five young children, and burdened with debt.

Ever since childhood Frank had been thinking up inventions: rotary motors, clocks, even a new approach to spelling the English language based on phonetics. Early in 1921 he undertook to convince his real-estate contacts to buy into his inventions, to help him develop and patent and market new products.

Frank tried. Although he could sell land, he couldn't sell his ideas. "I realized if I was ever going to do anything," he said, "I would have to do it myself. So I decided the simplest and cheapest thing to develop would be the frozen lollypop."

With help and encouragement from his wife, Mary, he returned to the project. He hoped to convince suppliers to give him discounted rates by offering them a percentage of his profits. He got replies such as "not in our line" (from an ice-cream maker) and "only a child's confection" and "never a commercial success." He struggled on. One supplier said no to the investment but introduced him to six-inch glass test tubes, the perfect mold.

Frank invented a machine to manufacture the treat. It

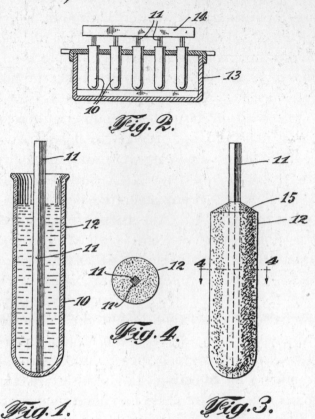

*The molds (Figs. 1 and 2) and finished product (Fig. 3) from Frank Epperson's 1924 patent*

was a tank into which he put rock salt and chunks of ice from the local ice plant, to create freezing salt brine. Into this he dipped racks of glass test tubes containing the liquid syrup. Quick-freezing was his objective. The advantage of saltwater was that it reached much lower temperatures than freshwater without solidifying. If the treat froze too slowly, the water component would ice up first and float to the top of the test tube and the heavier sugar and flavoring would drop to the bottom. The unfortunate result would be a "product highly flavored at the bottom [of the tube] and almost flavorless at the top," according to the inventor.

Later, in 1923, he had another idea: if he circulated the brine around the test tubes, the treats would freeze faster. He installed an electric motor in the tanks to accomplish this, and reduced the freezing time for the snacks from about six minutes to as little as two minutes. According to his son George: "Without realizing it, Pop had invented the first modern fast-freezing process and never thought to patent it." In 1925, Massachusetts inventor Clarence Birds-eye patented the fast-freezing process that soon after started a whole industry: frozen foods for grocery shoppers.

Frank set up equipment for every step of production. He even rigged an old, heavy-duty printing press to stamp his name on the wooden sticks. The wood was a problem, though—it had to be tasteless, but it also had to provide a surface textured enough to grip the treat tightly. He discovered that birch, poplar, and basswood worked best. Later, he settled on thin slabs of wood from a nearby match company. But Frank had troubles making a device to feed the sticks properly; his feeder kept jamming, and for a time it seemed that the development of his discovery was stuck on a stick.

Frank decided to abandon automated stick-feeders and move forward anyway. He and Mary had other worries. What if someone beat them to the idea? They paid a patent attorney $50 to start the patent process. Weeks later, the attorney explained his work required an additional $50. The Eppersons tried to find a partner, but no one was interested. Using their own dwindling funds, they were able to pay the lawyer, and on March 5, 1923, Frank filed his application at the Patent Office.

After lengthy review by patent examiners and several revisions to his original patent claim, Frank was at last rewarded. On August 19, 1924, he received patent

#1,505,592 for "a frozen confection of attractive appearance, which can be conveniently consumed without contamination by contact with the hand and without the need for a plate, spoon, fork, or other implement."

But Frank had not waited for the patent to come through before trying to sell the thing.

In the basement of his real-estate office he had set up headquarters for his frozen treat and out in the garage he installed industrial refrigeration machinery to produce the ice needed to mix with salt in making a slushy salt brine. The press that stamped the brand name on the stick took its place in the attic over his boys' bedroom. Frank ran the hand-fed, foot-powered machine himself. His son George remembers, "We would be lulled to sleep at night by the constant thumpety-thump, thumpety-thump, thumpety-thump."

The sweet icicle became a family project. Early in 1923, Frank and Mary introduced the confection at a formal Fireman's Ball at Neptune Beach in Alameda, California. But it was not until they walked through the crowds, eating sample snacks themselves, that they found any takers.

Was this treat for adults or for children? The proprietors at Neptune Beach were interested in the answer, too. The following day, they offered Frank and Mary free use of a concession stand. The next morning, the Eppersons decorated the stand with gaily colored homemade flags, and Mary and the children dressed in clown suits and walked about munching the dessert to entice passersby to try it.

Runaway success? That's the newspaper story. But the Epperson children tell a different tale. The overwhelming success was later. In the beginning, very few customers plunked down a dime for what the young family was working so hard to promote. Frank had assured the kids his idea was a "winner." What was wrong?

"I'd say it was table manners," says Frank's son John,

*The original Ep-sicle label*

who'd walked through the crowds as a child wearing a clown costume and licking the treat. "It was a different world then."

Gradually, demand grew for this informal treat. At state and county fairs and on the beaches, crowds of adults and children began clamoring for Frank's product. A name change helped. Frank's first name, Ep-sicle, fell by the wayside and was replaced by Popsicle.

How did this famous brand name originate? Some industry historians think the term was a combination of "soda pop" and "icicle." The Epperson children themselves have different memories. One traces it to the "pop" sound made from the vacuum suction when early frozen bars were pulled from their molds. John Epperson states that "Epsicle referred to frozen fruit bars full of chunks of pineapple and cherry. When we decided to make a clear fruit syrup bar, we needed another name. We all got in a huddle around the dinner table suggesting different names, and George said, 'I've got the idea, Pop, let's call it the Popsicle after you!' "

On May 26, 1923, Frank sold Eastern production rights to a New Jersey corporation, and on June 6, 1923, this company filed for the trademark rights in Washington, D.C. A trademark is the name, symbol, or slogan of a product that belongs only to the trademark owner. Like patents, trade-

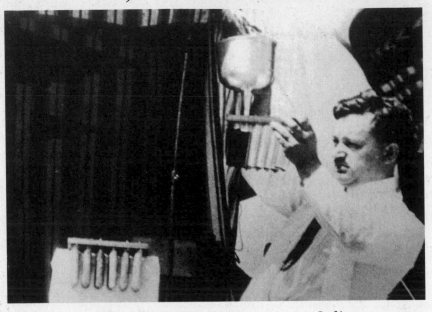

*Frank making his frozen treat at Salinas, California, in 1923*

marks are registered by the U.S. Patent and Trademark Office, but trademarks have no time limit to their exclusivity. Apparently, the inventor of the Popsicle never owned its trademark.

But Frank did engineer overwhelming success for his product across the country. A flood of orders kept him busy supplying equipment and syrup. "Your Popsicle," a man from New Jersey's Palisades Amusement Park wrote Frank, "is the only proposition that has ever returned its full investment cost in one day's operation." By 1928, Frank had earned royalties for the sale of over sixty million Popsicles.

Sadly, when the Great Depression arrived, Frank's involvement in real estate brought him close to bankruptcy. His boss and several friends committed suicide as disaster overtook many Oakland realtors. To raise money, Frank took a big step—he sold all his frozen-dessert rights to the Joe Lowe Corporation for $50,000. The money was split three ways: one-third to the man who had introduced him to Joe Lowe, one-third to the lawyer, and one-third to Frank himself.

"I had to liquidate," said the man who solidified the Popsicle.

Although Frank later regretted the sale, there was a positive side. The sale helped his family through hard times. And his idea was a triumph that is still part of our lives. When the Popsicle celebrated its fiftieth anniversary in 1973, Popsicle Industries announced that it had sold more than three billion desserts on a stick that year. During the anniversary, newspapers and magazines honored Frank as a truly important contributor to the American scene.

The idea of this eleven-year-old boy did not melt away.

BYPASS LINE    TRANSMISSION LINE
POWER LINE

# THOMAS EDISON
## LIGHTNING SLINGER

Imagine an invention. At first, you might think of some type of metal box crammed with gears and levers and wires, some type of *contraption*. But there's another side to invention that is recognized by the U.S. Patent and Trademark Office: inventions can be ingenious new *ways* of doing things.

In his lifetime, Thomas Alva Edison was granted 1,093 patents for his inventions, most of them *contraptions*. He is famous for inventing and developing the first commercially practical incandescent lamp or light bulb, the phonograph, the kinetoscope or peep-show machine, and many other devices that have permanently changed our world. Many people don't know, however, that his earliest invention was a *way* of doing something and that it came to pass before he'd reached the age of seventeen.

Growing up in the 1850s, Edison was a familiar figure in his hometown of Port Huron, Michigan. Everyone knew him as Al, and he had a reputation as a kid who always got into trouble. He had problems in school, and he had them at home, where, he recalled, his parents kept a birch whipping stick handy, with "the bark wore off."

Despite being an avid reader and experimenter, Al didn't do well in the classroom. He endured brief stints in two schools before his formal education came to an end. It just didn't work. As Al's father put it, "Teacher told us to keep him in the streets, for he would never make a scholar."

But Al's mother, a former schoolteacher, took her son in hand, keeping him busy at home with lessons and an extensive reading program. Inspired by some of the books he read, Al conducted experiments in chemistry, and tinkered with machines, reputedly building a miniature steam-powered sawmill and railroad.

Eventually, at twelve, Al found a job selling newspapers, apples, candy, and dime novels on the Grand Trunk Railroad.

There is a photo of Al from his railroad days. Viewers can see a smile on his face that spreads almost ear to ear. It is a smile that comes from deep within. Clearly, this kid had found what he liked. Looking back many years later, Edison himself wrote, "The happiest time in my life was when I was twelve years old."

The Grand Trunk traveled the sixty-three miles from Al's hometown to Detroit, leaving in the morning, returning in the evening. During the layover, Al had plenty of time on his hands. His refuge was the Detroit Young Men's Society library. He decided to continue his education by reading and tried to go through the shelves book by book. He didn't get very far, however, soon encountering books that he called "dry"—among them a volume on mathematics, a subject he thoroughly detested.

During breaks on the train, Al dabbled in chemical experiments in an empty car. A resulting fire, caused when a bottle of phosphorus broke on the floor, almost cost him his job. Around the same time, he also started a little newspaper, *The Weekly Herald*, which was produced on the train at first, and then in his attic at home. He was reporter, editor, publisher, and printer all in one. But his newspaper didn't sell enough copies, so he tried a scandal sheet, using

Paul Pry as his pen name. After a roughing up by the angry subject of one of his stories, though, Edison decided to quit the newspaper business.

Around this time, Al began losing his hearing. According to some biographers, it was the result of a childhood illness. Al blamed an incident in which a train employee, trying to bring him aboard a slowly moving baggage car, pulled him up by his ears. At first, Al said, he had an earache, "then a little deafness," then a gradual loss of hearing over the following months.

"I haven't heard a bird sing since I was twelve years old," he said later in some autobiographical notes. But he came to feel that his handicap had something to do with helping him become an inventor. Deafness forced him to concentrate. "In my isolation (insulation would be a better term) I had time to think things out."

At the age of fifteen, Al left the railroad. Candy-selling may have been fun, but the Grand Trunk didn't pay him any wages, allowing him instead a tiny profit on each item sold. Luckily, Al had landed a chance for a very promising new career. He became a telegrapher's apprentice.

Al received his training in Mount Clemens, Michigan, working under a young stationmaster named James Mackenzie. One day during his time as a candy vendor, Al had pulled Mackenzie's son out of the path of an oncoming train. In gratitude, Mackenzie had offered to teach Al his prestigious trade.

The electromagnetic telegraph was fairly new. In the 1830s Samuel Morse had designed a practical telegraphic communications system, and less than twenty years later it had spread across North America. The telegraph was a simple device that dispatched electrical impulses through wires which could be strung between cities, towns, and eventually nations. By interrupting the flow of current, the impulses could be made long or short. On this basis, Morse designed a code that is in use, with some modifications, to this day, assigning a combination of long and short signals to each letter of the alphabet.

At telegraph stations, the impulses passed through an electromagnet on a receiver, causing a lever to move against a sounding piece, tapping out the long and short signals; the process was reversed to send messages via a keypad. Telegraphers, or "lightning slingers," as they were known, had to translate these codes quickly into words, and vice versa. The job demanded sharp reflexes and fast thinking. The rewards were excellent wages and a glamorous image.

Al had been fascinated by telegraphy for years. When he was nine, his mother had given him Richard Green Parker's *School Compendium of Natural and Experimental Philosophy*, a favorite book that contained a section devoted to this exciting new technology. As a teenager, using a half mile of stovepipe wire, Al and a neighbor set up a line between their houses on which they could chatter back and forth into the night.

For one of his first lessons with Mackenzie, Al showed up with a telegraph set that he had made at a Detroit gunsmith's shop. He worked hard to hone his skills. According to the inventor, his deafness proved to be an advantage: "While I could hear unerringly the loud ticking of the instrument, I could not hear other and perhaps distracting sounds."

When Al sat down to telegraph messages, under his finger flowed the force that would lead to nearly a thousand of his adult inventions. Ironically, it was the absence of electricity that led to his kid invention.

After several months with Mackenzie, Al was given a job in his hometown as telegrapher at a jewelry and book store. One winter morning in early 1863, he arrived at work and discovered an emergency had arisen. The telegraphic cable across the St. Clair River between the United States and Canada had broken in the night. Ice floes had apparently ripped the cable loose, and they also made passage by ferry impossible.

What to do? The Canadians would be furious at this break in communications, especially investors, who depended on news of the Civil War, now in its second year.

Al had an idea. The young telegrapher contacted some workers at the Grand Trunk and a locomotive was pulled up on the tracks beside a dock on the river. Al joined the engineer in the locomotive cab. Soon the whistle sounded in a series of long and short toots. The short dots of the telegraphic code became quick blasts on the train whistle. The long dashes were signaled with drawn-out bleats.

Would the scheme work? Would some Canadian on the other side take down the message on paper, return to his station, and then, by telegraphy, speed the messages onward? A crowd gathered on the American side to view the unfolding drama. On the distant shore, Al saw figures scurrying back and forth. Next, a locomotive puffed up on the Canadian side and its whistle answered back in long and short toots. The telegraph operator and the train operators on the far shore had joined ranks with their counterparts in Port Huron.

Because of Al, news was flowing into Canada. The American crowd broke into applause.

His invention didn't last long, of course. It was a way of doing something that became obsolete as soon as the telegraph company repaired the cable. But it served a purpose, a very crucial one.

Later in his life, Edison would be widely celebrated as the Wizard of Menlo Park, his laboratory and home in New Jersey. But there in Port Huron on that cold morning, he had a taste of what it was like to be a wizard for a day.

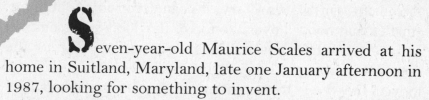

# MAURICE SCALES
## CLEARLY EXCELLENT

**S**even-year-old Maurice Scales arrived at his home in Suitland, Maryland, late one January afternoon in 1987, looking for something to invent.

At school that day, Maurice's teacher had announced an invention contest. There would be cash prizes. There would be a ceremony, where winning contestants would shake hands with one of the astronauts who had walked on the moon. All Maurice needed was an inspiration.

"He was trying to think up something helpful to other people," according to his mother, Candace. Inspiration came from an unexpected source. Maurice's baby sister, Amaleya, loved to toddle around the house. One of her favorite pastimes was closing open doors. The problem was that she couldn't reach the doorknobs, so her pudgy fingers wrapped around the edge of the doors, and when she closed them, she often slammed her fingers.

"What kind of invention would people be interested in?" Maurice wondered aloud as he ate his after-school snack.

"Well, look around," advised Candace Scales.

Maurice didn't have to look anywhere. There was a shriek as Amaleya pinched her fingers again, and just as suddenly Maurice had his idea. What about a device to solve his sister's problem, a device to keep the door from squeezing her fingers? According to Maurice, "The answer just came." A few minutes later he spread out drawing paper on the floor and penciled in the shape of the device he envisioned. Next he cut out the shape and began to experiment with different ways to bend and fold the paper. It was the beginning of the invention he would name Baby-No-Mash.

The first model he made was an inverted L. The problem? It pushed off the top of the door. He tried again. He glued and taped wood to the cardboard model for reinforcement. On the third try, he came up with something smaller that hooked over the top of the door—it resembled an inverted J. If he pushed the gadget near the edge of the door, away from the hinges, the door opened a crack. If he moved the thing toward the hinges, the door remained open several inches.

It was a simple and effective solution to a problem—no more tears from his sister.

Baby-No-Mash won the contest at his school. It advanced to triumph at the state level, and when the ten-state Southeastern Division of Invent America! announced its results, they named Maurice the winner in his age group, and he was chosen to compete at the national level. But somewhere along the way Baby-No-Mash needed one improvement. The problem was his cardboard prototype, which is what an original full-scale working model is called. Maurice's idea was fresh, but the cardboard was worn out.

Why not make a wooden prototype? Wood might withstand transporting and handling, but unfortunately Maurice didn't have the carpentry skills. At this point his Uncle Rhawn, a display maker at the Smithsonian Institution, learned of his difficulty and suggested Plexiglas, a kind of plastic that, because it is clear and can be shaped when hot, has found widespread use, from airplane windows to decorative objects. It was an ideal match of product and material.

With supervision from his uncle and his father, Maurice worked in his grandfather's back yard—only Grandfather Clarence had a vise heavy enough to hold the gadget. First, he taped the paper design onto the Plexiglas sheet. Then he sawed the plastic, using the edge of the paper for a guide. Some sanding with a power tool smoothed the edges. Next, he passed a blowtorch back and forth over the Plexiglas until it was soft enough to bend to just the shape needed.

When Maurice finished, he had a stronger version of his invention that was also attractive enough to market.

Although Baby-No-Mash didn't win at the national level, Maurice rang up his share of victories. In the weeks that followed, he was filmed for the local TV news, interviewed by newspapers, and featured in an article in *Ebony* magazine. His mom remembers that he and the other winners were awarded trips to the national banquet in Washington, D.C., where he received a $500 savings bond. He attended ceremonies with his family and his teacher, who managed to persuade George Bush, then Vice President, to autograph Maurice's cardboard prototype, a trophy the boy later hung proudly in his room. And to top it off, Maurice shook hands with an astronaut.

Many influences helped shape Maurice into a kid inventor. These include his Grandfather Clarence, who is himself a patented inventor; his teacher, Era Gilbert, whose students have won other national awards for inventive thinking and who set up an "Invention Center" in the middle of her schoolroom; and his mother and father, who encourage his creativity. But if you ask Maurice about the motive that led to Baby-No-Mash, he has a different answer.

"I wanted to see what I could do," he says.

# BENJAMIN FRANKLIN
## UNSINKABLE

**M**ost people know him as one of the Founding Fathers of our country, a diplomat, an author, a scientist. But by the time he reached twelve years of age, Ben Franklin was also a successful kid inventor.

Born in Boston in 1706, Ben grew up the youngest son in the family of Josiah Franklin, a soap and candle maker. Remarkably, for all his triumphs and the many pathways that opened before him later, Ben experienced a series of false starts in his early life. His father first wanted him to be a minister. Josiah dubbed his son the family "tithe," meaning that just as he offered up a tithe, or a tenth of his income, to the church, he would offer up his tenth and last son to the ministry. In 1714, Ben was sent to Boston Latin School, the first step that would lead to divinity studies at Harvard College.

At year's end, however, Josiah decided he didn't have enough money for Ben to continue. Next, Ben was enrolled in an arithmetic and writing school, an education more in keeping with his parents' social standing. Ben had some academic success, but he failed math. One year later, the family's budget pinched again and Josiah brought him home to work in the candle shop.

Ben loathed candle-making. In his *Autobiography*, he later grimly remembered his duties as "cutting Wick for the

Candles, filling the Dipping Mold, and the Molds for cast Candles, attending the Shop, going of Errands, & c."

Ben was a stout, strong kid with a pleasant, moon-shaped face. He had a good sense of humor, which he needed while his family played games with his future.

It wasn't just Ben's immediate family. There was Uncle Benjamin from England, who wrote silly amateur verses. He encouraged his American namesake to be a poet, and while not yet a teen, the boy published a ballad, based on a true story, about a husband, wife, and daughter drowning in Boston Harbor that "sold wonderfully," according to Franklin. Was this the career for Ben? Ben's father stepped in and said no. "Verse-makers are generally beggars," he advised. Then came Cousin Samuel, who tried to teach Ben his cutlery business, an unhappy and brief experiment.

In 1718, the family decided to apprentice Ben to his older brother James, who was a printer. In colonial America, apprentices served a master in exchange for learning a craft or trade, but the relationship of an apprentice to his master sometimes resembled that of a prisoner to his cell-keeper. Even though the contract Ben signed said he would obey James "day and night," they often quarreled. According to Ben, James sometimes beat him. "I think our Family," Ben later recalled, "were always subject to being a little Miffy."

Ben's kid inventions may have come about during moments stolen from the printshop. For some reason, Ben never mentioned his childhood inventions in the famous *Autobiography*. Luckily, in a 1773 letter to his old friend in France, Jacques Barbeu-Dubourg, Franklin took great pleasure in remembering them.

He was twelve, perhaps thirteen, and when he wanted to relax, he liked to go to a favorite spot called Mill Pond. Not far from Ben's front door, Mill Pond was a tidal cove with a dam across its mouth. Ben had excellent swimming skills. He had been reading books that explained new swimming techniques. He even devised a few of his own. The next step? Why not invent a *thing* to improve his swimming?

First, he invented hand paddles. "I made two oval palettes," he recalled, "each about ten inches long and six broad, with a hole for the thumb, in order to retain it fast in the palm of my hand. They much resembled a painter's palettes. In swimming I pushed the edges of these forward, and I struck the water with their flat surfaces as I drew them back. I remember I swam faster by means of these palettes, but they fatigued my wrists."

Next Ben made a pair of flippers for his feet. He described them as "a kind of sandals," but he abandoned the effort because he was not satisfied with the results.

It was his last water invention that was his best. One day at the pond, Ben loosed a large kite into the air and, holding onto the stick, walked into the water. "I found that lying on my back and holding the stick in my hands, I was drawn along the surface of the water in a very agreeable manner. Having then engaged another boy to carry my clothes round the pond, to a place which I pointed out to him on the other side, I began to cross the pond with my kite, which carried me quite over without the least fatigue, and with the greatest pleasure imaginable."

As an adult, Ben created many famous inventions, including the lightning rod, bifocal glasses, and the Franklin stove—an energy-efficient improvement on fireplace heating. He even devised a musical instrument, the glass harmonica, based on "the sweet tone that is drawn from a drinking glass, by passing a wet finger round its brim."

This great early American inventor had an interesting view about patents. In his *Autobiography*, he explains why he did not file for one on his stove. "As we enjoy great Advantages from the Inventions of others," he wrote, "we should be glad of an Opportunity to serve others by any Invention of ours."

# HANNAH CANNON

## BIG DEAL

When you hold a deck of playing cards, in your hand rests an invention more than a thousand years old. No one knows who first created playing cards, but their history stretches back to the parlors of European kings in the Middle Ages and beyond, all the way to the imperial courts of ancient China. In contrast to this mysterious and regal past, the most recent development in the history of playing cards took place in Hollywood Hills, California, in 1987.

Hannah Cannon, a freckled, redheaded eleven-year-old, was raised by her father on a street that TV and movie stars called home. Her main interest at the time was collecting posters of her favorite rock groups. "I never meant to be an inventor," remembers Hannah today. "It just popped into my mind. I get lots of little ideas."

Her brainstorm was to put the letters of the alphabet on a deck of cards, so she could play games as usual—except she would be making words for points.

"We had been into games," remembers her father, Bill Cannon, a professional screenwriter. "One evening we were watching television when suddenly she turned to me and said, 'Daddy, I think I've invented a game.'"

Hannah and Bill decided to try her idea. They inked letters onto the cards of a regular fifty-two-card deck. Then they assigned a point value to each letter, based on the difficulty of using that letter in a word, in comparison with other letters in the alphabet. "E" or "S" were given fewer points, for instance, than "X" or "Z."

Hannah didn't have to set many rules, because her games were simply variations on poker, rummy, war, and even solitaire. Instead of collecting pairs or flushes or suits, the players try to form words. For instance, in a game of poker the bidding goes back and forth as usual, but in Hannah's game players are betting on something new and special: who has the word or words worth the most points. In war, players still split the deck equally, but instead of laying down one card at a time, they lay down five. The object is to make a word worth more points than the other players' and capture upturned cards.

After some experimenting, Hannah and Bill decided a seventy-eight-card deck worked best. Then they created suits based on colors, including one suit of wild cards. Players receive extra points for making words with letters all of the same suit.

In searching for refinements, Hannah and Bill didn't have trouble finding "guinea pigs" to experiment on. Willing friends and guests found themselves playing the new game.

Hannah had figured out a brilliant yet logical way to combine word games like Scrabble and traditional cards. "It was a big idea," says Bill Cannon. So big, he reasoned, that someone must have dreamed it up before. He did a bit of research and checked to see if toy stores or catalogues carried a similar product. None did.

Encouraged, he had a talk with Hannah. "Do you really want to do this?" he asked. Yes, she did. And so, in the early months of 1988, a new game company was born— Hannah's Game Corporation.

They could not patent the idea because the U.S. Patent and Trademark Office does not protect games. But parts of a game can receive protection. Hannah could register the name of her invention as a trademark. Hannah and Bill picked CARDZ for the name of their product. In addition, after hiring an artist to design the new deck, they registered the look of her game with the U.S. Copyright Office. A copyright establishes that a piece of writing or a visual image belongs only to the owner of the copyright.

From the start, people were attracted to CARDZ. A graphics company gave the Hannah Game Corporation a $10,000 credit on printing the cards, in exchange for a share of future earnings. And as the news spread, the media rushed to tell Hannah's story. She found herself interviewed on *Good Morning America*. Her picture appeared in *People* magazine.

Hannah then went on to make toy-business history at the American International Toy Fair. This is an annual trade show where the makers of toys and games display new

*The CARDZ package design*

ideas to buyers for stores and catalogues. At the time, Toy Fair had one ironclad rule: it banned the general public and anyone under eighteen years of age. In 1990, Toy Fair made an exception to its rule. As the inventor of CARDZ, Hannah Cannon had the honor of being the first child ever permitted on the floor of the convention.

In the months that followed, CARDZ began to appear in stores. Waldenbooks, Bloomingdale's, and other outlets sent in orders as the demand grew. More than fifty thousand CARDZ were sold nationwide. Educators recognized teaching possibilities in this fun game based on word formation, and Bill put together and sold special CARDZ educational kits. One school professional remarked, "In thirty

*Hannah Cannon on* Good Morning America, *May 1988*

years as an educator, I have never seen a better educational tool."

Although CARDZ posted excellent sales for a time, several months later business went downhill. Hannah and Bill had sold mass-market rights to a company that specialized in toy start-ups. This company got the game on the shelves of Toys-R-Us and other national toy stores, but it changed the name on the package—a right the company did not legally possess. People who had seen Hannah on TV would come to a large toy store asking for CARDZ and would be sent away empty-handed because the employees were unaware of the name change. Eventually, the Cannons recovered all the market rights, but in 1991 Hannah told her father she "was tired of being famous." Perhaps the stresses of marketing schedules and being a "spokeschild" to the media were too much. Without hesitation, Bill closed up operations.

There is still a demand for CARDZ, but Hannah and Bill are holding it off the market until they find a bigger toy or game company to take it on. Bill has studied the history of other famous games and knows that CARDZ could be an even bigger hit the second time around. And Hannah, who is now in college, remembers the early days of the game with pleasure. "It's fun to think that people liked playing it," she says. "It's cool."

# Robert Goddard
## BLASTING OFF

**K**id inventors have had their share of duds.

Lionel Cowan, the inventor of the toy electric train, was trying to invent a mini-locomotive when he was six years old. As he attached a tiny steam motor to a locomotive he'd carved from wood, the device exploded. Fortunately, Lionel didn't blow any fingers off.

The Wright brothers first tried to fly as kid inventors. In 1878 their father gave them the latest rage in flying toys, a tiny helicopter made in France that was propelled by a rubber band. Soon the Wright boys were asking, why not increase the size of the machine to make it big enough to carry real passengers aloft? They tried but failed.

Another famous inventor who faced failure as a kid experimenter is Robert H. Goddard, now regarded as the father of space flight. The story of his childhood persistence is amazing.

Growing up in the 1880s in a Boston suburb, Goddard showed an early interest in flight. At five, having observed that shoes scuffed on carpet produced sparks, and that batteries produced electricity, he tried to combine the two effects. Using a zinc rod from a battery, he rubbed zinc on the soles of his shoes. Then, in hopes of creating sparks big enough to bounce him into the air, he scuffed along the pavement and jumped repeatedly from a low fence. His mother intervened and quickly put a stop to the experiment. But, clearly, here was a kid who wanted to get off the ground.

Goddard had many bouts with sickness in his youth, including bronchitis and pleurisy, an inflammation of the lungs. During one of his illnesses, he holed up with the science-fiction yarn *From Earth to the Moon*, by Jules Verne. To most readers, this story of space travel was strictly fantasy, but to Goddard it contained real possibilities. In the margins of the book, he scribbled notes on how to make Verne's ideas work, or to point out when Verne was taking liberties with scientific fact.

Goddard may have learned from his father to believe in the possibilities of invention. Nahum Goddard was a co-owner of a machine-knife factory. He had invented a rabbit knife, for cutting rabbit fur in the apparel industry. Once he saw that his son might follow in his footsteps, Nahum encouraged Robert by subscribing to general-interest science magazines, buying technical books, and giving him money for items used in the small experiments he conducted in an attic laboratory.

One such experiment was an attempt to create artificial diamonds. But when Robert was heating a glass tube of hydrogen gas over a flame in his attic lab, the glass exploded. A fierce concussion shot a piece of glass, with the cork attached, into the ceiling and embedded it there; flying bits of glass dented the door; and some shards actually ended up on the second story below. The boy emerged unscathed, but as he says in some autobiographical notes, "the servant girl, who was in the room opposite, screamed that she was killed, until assured by the family that she was not."

Despite his interest in science, Goddard had problems

with school. At the age of fifteen, he took the entrance exam to the prestigious Roxbury Latin School, along with his friends, but failed. Perhaps his illnesses had caused him to miss too many schooldays. In an attempt to restore him to health, Nahum probably kept up their habit of taking country walks. "My father and I were great pals," the inventor later said. They went tramping the back roads of Massachusetts, hunting, fishing, and experimenting with photography.

In 1898, the *Boston Post* published daily excerpts from H. G. Wells's *The War of the Worlds* (adapted to make Boston the setting, rather than London). The story of Martians in metal containers invading our planet "gripped my imagination tremendously," said Goddard. If Wells could imagine ways for Martians to travel here, why couldn't Robert, by the same logic, think of ways for us to travel there?

During this period, Goddard made a homemade bow and arrow. Or was it? He didn't put feathers on his shaft to balance the arrow for shooting at targets. He wrapped copper wire around the stem for vertical balance, shaved a lead tip to the shape of a bullet, and tried to shoot straight up as high as possible. The sky was beckoning.

In the winter of 1897–8, he decided to make a self-propelled flying machine. His first thought was a craft with motor-driven propellers, but for some reason he considered only electricity as a workable power source, and he had to abandon the concept because the batteries would weigh too much. He settled for a balloon, but with a difference—one made from aluminum: "a small balloon, attached to a thread and 'flown' like a kite."

Scientists had experimented with the intriguing metal called aluminum for more than half a century. But production methods that made pure aluminum widely available had been patented only recently. Scouring the industrial-supply shops, Robert found a small company in the Boston area which sold him a quarter-pound bar. He immediately saw the importance of this lightweight metal to flight. At a time when adult inventors had not figured this out, decades before aluminum alloys were in extensive use in the aeronautics industry, a kid inventor in his family attic was trying to make an aluminum flying machine.

The idea was brilliant. The results, not so brilliant. Aluminum proved difficult to shape and fashion. Goddard wrote in his journal on January 8, 1898: "Tried to melt it nearly all-day but could not." Finally, he obtained some sheet aluminum one-hundredth of an inch thick and bent it to form a pillow shape, which he then cemented shut with litharge, a powder containing lead, and glycerin, a solvent.

Robert showed the neat drawings he had made to guide his aluminum work to a friend who worked at the local druggist's. The boy was impressed and helped Robert obtain the tank of hydrogen gas the experiment needed.

On February 19, 1898, Robert and his friend set forth to launch the flying machine from a sidewalk on Dudley Street, outside the drugstore. Robert attached a tube from the hydrogen tank to an opening in the side of the balloon; his friend manned the tank's valve. That night Robert wrote in his journal, "Aluminum balloon will not go up . . . Aluminum is too heavy. Failior [*sic*] crowns enterprise."

That year was a terrible year for the Goddard family. His mother, Fanny Louise, had been very ill, and now physicians diagnosed her disease as tuberculosis. In 1899, the family decided to move to the country. Nahum sold their large home and his share in the knife company.

The Goddards moved into the second story of a farmhouse outside Worcester that belonged to Robert's grandmother. It was a far cry from living in their own house, with servants, but Robert didn't seem to mind. A barn workshop proved an education in itself for him. The downstairs tenant taught him to use his tools and became such a good friend Robert called him Uncle George. Sometimes Robert would stare at the neatly arranged and well-oiled tools, and the vision was, he says in his memoirs, "an unending feast to my eyes."

On the afternoon of October 19, 1899, Robert had a pivotal experience. He had climbed the tall cherry tree at the back of the barn, carrying a saw to trim the dead branches. "It was one of the quiet, colorful afternoons of sheer beauty which we have in October in New England," he wrote later, "and as I looked toward the fields at the east, I imagined how wonderful it would be to make some device which had even the *possibility* of ascending to Mars, and how it would look on a small scale, if sent up from the meadow at my feet."

He would remember every detail of the scene for the rest of his life. "I was a different boy when I descended the tree." The date became so important to him that he always referred to it as Anniversary Day.

Continued poor health kept Robert out of school for two years after the move to Worcester. When he entered the local high school in 1901, he resolved to work especially hard in mathematics, which had always been his worst subject. He created his own little book of geometrical propositions and tried to prove them. This activity seemed to make math click for him, and by the end of the year, Goddard had advanced to the top of his math class.

While still a high-school sophomore, he submitted an article to *Popular Science News* on "The Navigation of Space." In the article he discusses problems in some popular notions of how man might ascend into space, such as the idea of using "the recoil of a gun placed in a vertical position with the muzzle directed downwards, to raise itself together with a car containing the operator." But the *Popular Science News* editors rejected the article.

Soon after graduating from high school, Robert reviewed his densely scribbled journals, which contained some pretty wild ideas. At one point, for instance, he had thought of using centrifugal force to power vehicles leaving the earth. But although wild ideas sometimes lead to breakthroughs, Robert decided the journals were "erroneous" and burned them.

In less than two months, however, he caught himself scribbling down more ideas for space travel. He dashed to a stationery shop and bought some green cloth-covered notebooks. Not just a few—a whole stack, enough to last for years. He was going all the way this time.

Eventually, Robert succeeded in becoming an aerospace pioneer. After moving on to Worcester Polytechnic, he became interested in the idea of linking two or more rockets

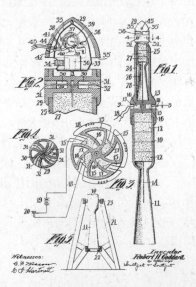

*Robert Goddard's first rocket patent*

together as a means of achieving high-altitude flight. In his first patent, filed in 1913, when he was thirty years old, he demonstrated the results of years of brilliant research and hard work. Among the significant aspects of this first patent were a design for firing "a secondary rocket when the explosive in the primary rocket is substantially consumed," and a tapered chamber at the end of the rocket that increased the thrust of the "gaseous products of combustion."

But it was in his green notebooks that Robert found the key to outer-space flight. In 1909, he began making notes about liquid fuels being preferable to the available solid fuels for powering rockets into space. After a decade of experiments with solid fuels convinced him of their limitations, he started working exclusively with liquid fuels. In 1926, Robert made aeronautical history by launching the first liquid-fuel-propelled rocket, using a combination of gasoline and liquid oxygen. Many more important achievements were to come. Ultimately, more than two hundred patents were awarded to him for his inventions. As an aerospace researcher, Robert succeeded to the point where one observer said it was impossible "to design a rocket, construct a rocket, launch a rocket, guide a rocket, or fly in space without infringing a Goddard patent."

Robert Goddard's persistence in the face of failure and frustration as a kid inventor led to eventual success as an adult. And his notebooks filled with wild, "erroneous" ideas turned out to be the launching pad for space flight.

# RALPH SAMUELSON
## THE DAREDEVIL

The place didn't have the dignity of a landmark in the history of invention—a small spit of sand, clouded with mosquitoes, the air hazy with early summer, a crowd of teenagers hooting and jeering. At the water's edge stood a boy with a rope. He was Ralph Samuelson, age eighteen. The place was Lake Pepin, a naturally occurring lake on the Mississippi River.

Growing up in nearby Lake City, Minnesota, Ralph had spent many hours around this waterfront. When Minnesota winters took hold, Ralph ventured out on the lake in an iceboat. He also scooted down the river bluffs on snow skis, and during the winter of 1922 it was snow skis, as he recalled in later interviews, that gave him his great inspiration.

"I decided that if you could ski on snow," said Ralph, "you could ski on water."

His reasoning didn't convince his friends. As he got ready to experiment with the device he called "water skis," word spread quickly around town and the beach overflowed with kids. They came to laugh. See Ralph put on his snow skis on a hot June day. See Ralph holding onto a rope behind his big brother Ben's powerboat. See Ralph sink. The first experiment was a total failure.

"Young punks"—that's how Ben Simons, who was seven years old at the time, described himself and the others who jammed the Lake City Marina. "Everyone in town thought it was a kind of joke."

Perhaps the laughter hardened the determination of the Minnesota teenager. Ralph returned day after day, trying to accomplish the feat, and just as regularly an audience gathered on the shore, ready to howl with laughter when he came up short. But the sturdy kid known as the town daredevil was a determined thinker, who always returned to the lake with a revised experiment based on lessons learned from the previous day's failure.

When snow skis flopped, he switched to barrel staves. When that didn't work, he tried skiing on pine boards, eight feet long and nine inches wide, with tips he had curled up by softening them in his mother's wash boiler and then clamping them in vises. After sinking a few times on these, Ralph was in a smashup from which he barely escaped uninjured.

Next, Ralph visited a blacksmith and had metal reinforcements made for where the first set of planks had cracked. There was a rational process here—and sometimes an irrational one, too. Ralph confessed to labeling his experimental skis "left" and "right." "Somehow they worked better that way," he said.

His vision of zooming over the lake surface was simple. The solution proved complex. He decided boat rope was too heavy and began using a hundred-foot length of window-sash cord. Another trip to the blacksmith gave him an iron ring which he tied to the cord as a handle. Then he wrapped the ring in rubber to give himself a better hold.

How to start? A series of experiments led him to the answer. He tried to step off the side of the boat, one ski at a time. Another approach was a deep-lake start with only his head bobbing above the surface. Finally, he discovered "sitting" in the deep with his ski tips poking out of the water in front of him.

Every failure brought him closer. At last, on July 2, 1922, his improvements led to success: a few yards flying atop the lake. By then, the kids on the shore were on Ralph's side; his persistence had made him a hero. "It was really a thrill when he finally did get up and go," says Ben Simons.

During that first summer, Ralph put on demonstrations that delighted the spectators. Articles appeared in the local newspapers. Thousands of people flocked to the beach to

Two Thousand People See Ralph Samuelson Perform Behind Seaplane

Photo by St. Paul Pioneer Press.

Last Sunday afternoon at the Lake City bathing beach 2,000 people were given a real thriller when Ralph Samuelson of this city did water skiing behind a seaplane that sped through the water at a dizzy pace and at times flew a few feet above the water. Ralph Samuelson again demonstrated his right to be termed "the best water ski rider in the Northwest" by his performance Sunday afternoon. People from Rochester, Red Wing, Wabasha and many other cities were in attendance to witness the water sports program of which the water skiing was the outstanding feature.

Water sports programs such as the one of last Sunday have done much to make the Lake City bathing beach one of the most popular recreation centers in southern Minnesota. Indications are that the attendance at the Lake City bathing beach next summer will far exceed that of this year.

*From the* Wabasha County Leader, *August 28, 1925*

watch. Ralph performed Sunday-afternoon shows and charged admission. He donated the proceeds to the town, keeping just enough pocket money to pay for the power-boat's gasoline.

In the fall of 1926, Ralph drove down to Palm Beach, Florida, where he began staging one-man water shows. With five summers of practice under his belt, he had added new tricks—skiing on one foot, riding onto a partly sub-merged lard-greased float to launch himself into a sixty-foot jump, balancing on one ski in a headstand. Ralph had even zipped along attached to a World War I seaplane at speeds up to 80 m.p.h. Now, his dangerous feats stunned and amazed the Florida tourists. He was a professional showman.

His career lasted into the late thirties (some accounts say late twenties) and came to an end because of back injuries suffered while he was working part-time in construction at a Palm Beach boat livery. Curiously, he had no school of students eager to imitate him, and just as curiously, he was never seriously injured during his ski shows. "The good Lord must have been watching over me," Ralph com-mented. But by 1937 his waterskiing days were over, and he vanished from the public eye, unacknowledged as the in-ventor of a new sport.

In 1963, an alert newspaperwoman from St. Paul, on vaca-tion at Lake City, saw Ralph's original skis displayed on the wall of a bathhouse on Lake Pepin. They were worn with time, as mysterious as two totems on a Pacific atoll. A hand-lettered card proclaimed: "World's First Water Skis." Newswriter Margaret Crimmins had heard of a continuing controversy over the origins of waterskiing. Some experts gave credit to a Long Island man who first skied in 1924. Some gave credit to the French, who popularized the sport in the late 1920s. (In Florida, Ralph had introduced French tourists to his innovation, which might explain how it crossed the ocean.)

Crimmins began making inquiries, rummaging through the yellowing pages of old issues of the local newspaper, where she discovered what had happened at the beach in 1922. She also discovered that no one knew if Ralph Samuelson was still living.

Margaret Crimmins then went home and wrote a column about Ralph in her paper, the *St. Paul Pioneer Press.* She asked, "Where are you now, Mr. Samuelson? I wish I knew. So do Ben Simons and a lot of other Lake Cityites who are proud of their native son."

The object of the search was living a mere thirty miles from the beach where he made history. Ralph had retired in Pine Island, Minnesota, after careers as a turkey farmer and as a state highway department worker. When a local druggist spotted the article and brought it to his attention, Ralph got in touch with Crimmins. Interviewed by the newswoman in St. Paul, Ralph spent hours describing his exploits and sharing his scrapbooks.

In January 1966, the American Water Ski Association officially recognized Ralph Samuelson as the Father of Water Skiing. For the last years of his life, he found himself in constant demand as guest of honor at water-ski shows and water-sport conventions. After his death in 1977, the state of Minnesota erected a stone marker on the shore of Lake Pepin in Ralph's memory, and the Water Ski Hall of Fame in Winter Haven, Florida, now displays his skis.

Today, more than seventeen million water-skiers in the United States alone enjoy a sport that began because of Ralph Samuelson's ingenuity and determination.

# Mary Spaeth
## A Fresh Approach

In 1966, Mary Spaeth—inventor, wife, and expectant mother—hit upon one of the remarkable inventions of our era. Working at Hughes Aircraft in Culver City, California, Mary became the inventor of tunable dye lasers. Lasers produce intense beams of light. Tunable dye lasers can be tuned to produce light at any color of the visible spectrum, and they have many scientific and medical applications. They've been used in eye surgery and are an important tool for scientists who are studying the nature of atoms, molecules, and crystalline materials. They are also a critical piece of hardware in systems designed to process materials such as uranium fuel for electric power reactors. With help from a tunable dye laser, astronomers will soon be able to use earth-based telescopes to see the stars nearly as well as they can from space with the Hubble telescope.

Although recently opportunities for women in technical careers have grown, in the 1960s only two percent of all patents were awarded to women. Often people ask Mary how she managed to become a high-tech inventor at that time. The answer starts with the story of her kid invention in Houston, Texas, during the 1940s.

When Mary Spaeth was three years old, her father, who

was an insurance salesman and an amateur handyman, brought home a jigsaw. "I sorta took charge of it," says Mary. During her preschool years, with the strong encouragement of her father, Mary had learned to use it and other tools as well. Before she was born, Mary's father had hoped for a girl he could raise as a tomboy. "And I lived up to his wildest dreams," Mary explains with a gleam in her eyes.

She had a workshop set up in the corner of the family's tiny one-car garage. "The most special present I ever got was a toolbox," she says, recalling a gift from her father when she turned six. "I still have many of those tiny tools and I still use the little hammer regularly." But it was in the kitchen and not in the garage that Mary's first invention came to be.

A bowl of cereal began the chain of events one morning. The cereal was stale—nothing like the exciting breakfast promised by the advertisers on the children's radio shows of that era.

"Soggy cereal," comments Mary. "That annoyed me. So I tried to figure out how I could fix that, right?"

Cold, ready-to-eat breakfast cereal was invented around the turn of the century. Radio advertising that started in the 1930s increased its popularity, especially among children. But for all the advances in the form of new flavors and new brands, cereal makers had not yet marketed boxes with resealable tops. The flaps on the tops of the boxes were glued shut, and to get inside a new box, consumers had to rip the lid. Then, because it was impossible to close the ripped lid, the cereal became stale and soggy, especially during the humid summers of southern Texas, near the Gulf of Mexico.

That morning, using the kitchen table as her laboratory, Mary tried to find a solution to the problem. With a sharp workshop knife instead of scissors (which would have nibbled out messy edges in the cardboard), she painstakingly separated the two glued flaps on the top of a new cereal box. Then, in her first attempt, she made a slit-and-tongue design, with a thin slice in one top flap corresponding to a notch protruding from the other.

At the age of eight, this kid inventor had created the resealable cereal box.

Although for years thereafter Mary carefully doctored the tops of cereal and cracker boxes to make them resealable, the idea of applying for a patent never occurred to her or to her parents. " 'Patent' was not a word that ever appeared in conversation in our house," she says. Neither Mary nor her encouraging dad and her tolerant mom ever thought of her activities as inventing.

Mary came up with her idea in 1946. It wasn't until the sixties that cereal manufacturers marketed boxes with a similar design. The cereal companies developed the idea on their own, and Mary didn't make any money from her inspiration. Today, packaging specialists call this design the "tuck-tab."

When Mary spotted the "new" box top on grocery shelves, she noted that the cardboard tongue she had designed was longer than the one the cereal makers were using, and, as a result, hers worked better.

What was her first reaction when she saw the newly designed cereal box on the shelves?

"It took them long enough."

# GEORGE WESTINGHOUSE
## STEAMING AHEAD

Soon after the Revolutionary War, American industries began to make increasing use of steam power. It was the era of rapid change known as the Industrial Revolution. Inventors came up with steam-powered machines that could manufacture more items than ever before, and they put together steam-powered vehicles—most important, the locomotive and steamship—that moved faster than man had ever dreamed.

In nineteenth-century America, however, there were no brakes to match the new high-speed engine technology. The brake system on a steam locomotive in the 1850s required a crew of five or six men to operate and could miss the stopping point by several thousand feet. It was as if all the thousands of inventors, mechanics, shops, and foundries across the nation were driven by a spirit that said "Go," and did not put as much thought into "Stop."

The results of this oversight were sometimes catastrophic. In 1856, the famous "Angola Horror" railroad accident near Philadelphia left sixty dead and more than that number severely injured when an excursion train loaded with children had a head-on collision with another train, a disaster that modern brakes might have averted.

In 1868, when he'd not yet reached his twenty-second birthday, George Westinghouse came to the rescue when he applied for the first of several patents on an automatic air brake. It was an inspiration that would lead him to fame and fortune.

The term "air brake" would seem to mean a system in which air pressure is used to force the brake on. This was the case in the first version of the Westinghouse system. But in one of his early refinements to the invention, George realized the advantages of using air pressure to keep the brakes off. As the air pressure drops, the brakes ease on. So, if one of the compressed-air lines breaks or leaks, or the steam compressor that supplies the system fails, the brakes *lock on*—a nifty safety feature. This basic system still operates today in trains, buses, and trucks.

When George was growing up in Schenectady, New York, he liked to watch skilled craftsmen at work, especially the employees at his father's factory turning out agricultural and mill machinery, and small steam engines. George himself was always whittling little gadgets from factory scraps. He was so devoted to these projects that once he started, he would skip school to finish them. No records exist of exactly what George whittled, but boys in that time often made pinwheels from sappy, pliable woods or from shingles. Put a wooden pinwheel in front of a jet of steam and the result is a primitive motor. Add a wheel with notches that engages notches in the shaft of the pinwheel; the result is increased power. George probably tinkered with such devices.

What did the young inventor's father, George Westinghouse, Sr., think of these experiments? The father called them "trumpery." He had other plans for his son. He wanted George to become a lawyer, a doctor, or a statesman. And the path to those careers lay in the classroom.

George Sr. was himself an inventor. One of his ideas, a scheme for an improved threshing machine (a device that separates grain from the husks and straw), had enabled him to set up his Schenectady shop. But he wanted George to rise above the manufacturing world.

As more absences were reported at school, his father forbade George to enter the shop during school hours. Battles must have resulted. Through the generations, the Westinghouse family has passed down memories of the father chasing his son around in circles, trying to whip him with a birch stick. Although the father seemed to rule in these disagreements, in the long run young George won. At thirteen, he started as a summer worker in his father's shop. But, existing employee records reveal, George soon began to put in workdays during the school term. Finally, school dropped off altogether. George was where he wanted to be.

In addition to performing his shop duties, George found time to use the tools and equipment for his own projects. He learned to work with metal as well as wood. His father tossed his creations into the factory scrap heap, but a sympathetic fellow employee set George up in a little den in the shop attic where he could continue working.

In 1861, at fifteen years of age, after experimenting on steam engines created by his father's workers, George came up with one of his own design. He invented a rotary steam engine. Many nineteenth-century inventors thought up designs for steam engines. Most of these engines were the reciprocating type—when the piston that drove the engine moved, it came to a stop, and its inertia had to be overcome for the next stroke. Some inventors asked, why not move the piston continuously in one direction, so there would be no energy loss from the piston changing direction? The pistons in George's rotary steam engine did just that. They were contained in a cylinder that formed a ring around the inside of a wheel "which is made to revolve about a hollow stationary shaft, through the opposite ends of which the steam is admitted and exhausted," according to the inventor.

George was so pleased with his own version of the rotary engine that he gave a public demonstration. Using metal from his father's workshop, he made a small model, attached it to a toy boat, and ran it successfully on the nearby Erie Canal to well-deserved applause from admiring onlookers.

When the Civil War broke out, George tried to enlist but was stopped by his father. Two years later, he joined with his father's blessing, serving in the army cavalry and later in the navy, as an engineering officer, and there he had the chance to think about powering real boats.

After the war, the old family battles still raged. Westinghouse, Sr., had not given up his plans for his son's future and enrolled him in Union College in Schenectady. It was a time when higher education was a formal affair. Students wore jackets, cravats, and silk shirts to class. But while the other students copied what the teacher said in his lecture, George inked designs for engines on his shirt cuffs.

On October 31, 1865, at age nineteen, George obtained a patent for the rotary steam engine he had designed as a kid. After this official recognition of his mechanical abilities, he must have been even less interested in pursuing a formal education. George Sr. finally relented. At Christmas break, on the recommendation of the school president, he withdrew his son from Union College and let him come to work in the shop.

George was never able to find a practical commercial application for his rotary steam engine, but he enjoyed tinkering with the invention throughout his life. And his

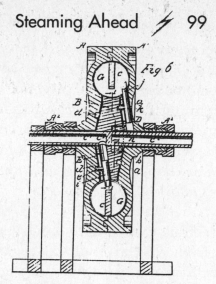

*Drawing from George Westinghouse's patent for a rotary steam engine*

work on the rotary engine laid the foundation for the very important work he did later in developing the turbine generator, a steam-, water-, or air-powered engine that produces electricity.

The modest income from his next invention—a device for putting derailed cars back on the track—enabled the twenty-year-old to marry and set out on a full-time career as an entrepreneur and inventor. But success did not come easy. After George invented his air brake, he struggled to convince people that the idea would work. Eventually, he found one railroad official who agreed to make available a train of cars for a public demonstration. According to one account:

*An air-pump driven by a small steam-engine was mounted on the locomotive, and air was compressed to sixty or seventy pounds per square inch. A pipe leading from the reservoir to a valve mechanism near the engineer's seat passed beneath the train to the brake-cylinders, one for the tender [the coal car] and one for each car. The piston of each brake-cylinder was connected to the ordinary hand-brake gear. Flexible hose connections were provided between the cars. To set the brakes, the engineer turned the valve so as to admit air to the pipe-line and brake-cylinders. The admission of air thrust out the pistons and set the brakes. To release the brakes, the engineer turned the valve so as to cut off connection with the main reservoir, and at the same time open the train pipe and cylinders to the outside atmosphere.*

The invention didn't take long to prove itself. Only a few hundred yards from where it had started, the demonstration train suddenly jerked to a halt. A wagon driver had fallen into the train's path at a crossing, and the engineer was forced to activate the new brakes. The train stopped within feet of the wagon driver and George had dramatic evidence of the capability of his innovation.

He went on to give successful demonstrations in Philadelphia, Chicago, St. Louis, and abroad. By 1871, he was working on his ingenious refinement to his original design, and a decade later his brake was installed on nearly seven thousand locomotives and thirty thousand cars in this country and others. By 1893, when Congress passed the Railroad Safety Appliance Act, air brakes had become mandatory equipment for trains.

George went on to other triumphs in a career that resulted in 361 patents and the establishment of more than fifty companies, among them Westinghouse Electric. At the time that George started working with electrical devices, the electrical current of choice was direct current, known as DC (electrical current flowing in one direction in a circuit). Later some inventors opted for a system known as alternating current, or AC (electrical current reversing itself many times per second in a circuit). The bitter struggle that ensued between companies and inventors devoted to one system or the other became known as the "Battle of the Currents." George invented devices that made alternating electrical current safe and led the AC campaign to victory—the result is the electrical system that we use today.

As George Westinghouse, Sr., had already learned, the person who invented the air brake could not be stopped.

# Johnnie Appleby

## A KNOTTY PROBLEM

It all started on a Saturday morning in a wheat field with a fifteen-year-old boy. The boy was John Francis Appleby, a sturdy farm kid who had a knack for fixing broken machines. After his father's death when he was seven, the boy's mother had been unable to support him. He'd moved from farm to farm, working to earn his room and board.

On that eventful morning, the kid known as Johnnie joined a cluster of farmers watching a horse-drawn mechanical grain cutter, or reaper, mow a field. This was a sales demonstration, and the proud salesman loudly boasted about his new machine. But even while the man spoke, Appleby was thinking the harvester needed one as yet uninvented attachment to make it as wonderful as the salesman claimed.

In that year, 1855, more than ninety percent of the people in the United States worked on farms. Each year, the prairies produced more grain. Each year, more American boats exported this grain across the oceans to people in other countries, bolstering the young nation's economy.

But American wheat farmers faced a problem which the increasing harvests made even worse. Although they had huge machines for cutting, described by one observer as a "cross between a metal monster and a wind-mill," the most exhausting job of all was still done by hand—raking the wheat together and tying it in bundles. It was "a back-breaking process," commented Appleby in a 1917 interview with a journalist.

Reapers that could rake the cut wheat into piles were eventually introduced. But no one had figured out how to make a machine that could tie a knot in twine to bind the wheat into a bundle. The Wisconsin newspaper editor S. D. Carpenter wrote editorials asking inventors to come forward with a solution. Across the nation, professional inventors worked on the puzzle. One adult inventor thought up an idea so complicated he needed thirty-five diagrams to explain it.

"I began to dream of a binding machine," Appleby told his interviewer. "I dreamed of it at night and I dreamed of it during the day." That morning in 1855 had gotten him started. The idea excited him so much that the normally shy kid spoke aloud: "Why not build a reaping machine that would bind the wheat into sheaves, too?" The men laughed at him. Everyone knew that it couldn't be done because of the knot. Up and down the Rock River Valley, people laughed at "Johnnie's knot."

But Johnnie was undaunted. One day two years later, while the teenager was working on a farm near Whitewater, Wisconsin, he hit upon an ingenious solution as he watched a little girl play with her puppy. At one point, she dropped her jumping rope over the pup's head like a leash collar, and the little dog shook itself free. As the rope slipped clear of the dog, it dropped to the ground in a knot. Later, while hoeing, Johnny became so excited thinking about the dog and the knot that he dropped his hoe and dashed to a nearby tree. On the spot, from a limb of the tree, he carved a model of the device that would tie knots.

What did it look like? Johnnie called his invention the "bird-bill knotter." It resembled the neck, head, and beak of

*A later version of the bird-bill knotter*

a bird. By laying two ends of a length of twine over the bird bill and then manipulating the bird bill through a series of specific movements, including rotating it completely around on its neck or shaft, Johnnie could make the device tie the two ends together in a simple overhand knot.

He didn't have enough money to file for a patent for this device or to fight off patent thieves in court, but Johnnie used his hard-earned savings to commission a gunsmith to fashion a metal model from his carving. And then he put the model away in an attic, his project halted by another interruption—the Civil War.

When Johnnie returned from duty in the Union Army a few years later, he set up a machine shop with a partner. He may have pushed his invention to the back of his mind, because during this time an inventor named Charles B. Withington seemed to have found the solution: a machine that could bind the wheat using *wire*. Withington sold half the rights for this device to Cyrus McCormick, the great inventor whose breakthrough reaper was widely used. McCormick's Chicago factories began to produce reapers with wire binders attached.

But there were problems. When the binder cut the wire, small bits of metal remained in the grain, and sometimes cattle and horses died from eating the fragments. Cattlemen called this "hardware disease." And flour mills had some disasters, too. In the mills, flour dust hung so thickly in the warm air that it was combustible. When bits of wire in the flour hit against rapidly moving metal parts in the milling machines, sparks were emitted and the result was sometimes an explosion. A storm of controversy arose over the health hazards caused by wire binders.

What to do? A machine that used wire had advantages— wire was stiff, easy to control, and needed only to be hooked or twisted together rather than knotted. Twine was biodegradable and digestible and wouldn't cause explosions, but was much trickier to work with, and the country needed an inventive genius who could tame it. So the great problem turned out not to have been solved after all.

In the spring of 1874, Johnnie thought back to his boyhood inspiration and talked the business partners in his machine shop and some friends into giving him financial backing.

Johnnie started to build the "invention" in the garret above his machine shop. But the glimmer that came to him in seconds when he was fifteen years old took three years to make into a reality. The centerpiece of the machine was his kid invention, but he had to attach his device to a working reaper. He had to build various arms and levers to gather the cut wheat into a sheaf, carry twine around the bundle, knot and cut the twine, and toss off the tied bundle. He had to devise the means for some forty separately moving parts to run off the turning of a single wagon axle. He

*An Appleby twine binder of 1880*

had to build a machine that wouldn't falter in wet grain or when it jiggled over broken ground.

By 1875, Johnnie was demonstrating a successful twine-binding harvester in the fields. Even then, however, success didn't come easy. Although he applied for a patent on February 27, 1877, his plans were so complicated that the Patent Office took until February 18, 1879, to finish reviewing them and recognize his claim.

Other obstacles arose. The companies that made harvesters had an investment in wire binders and didn't want any part of Appleby's inventions. But a young entrepreneur from Chicago came to see Appleby's demonstrations. In William Deering, Johnnie later recalled, "I found a man farsighted enough to see the importance of my inventions. To him belongs the credit of forcing my binder onto the market."

In the year that followed, Deering stunned the farming world when his relatively unknown company introduced three thousand twine-binding harvesters ready to roll. This was the machine farmers had wanted, and now it was available for them to buy. And buy it they did. Deering sold every harvester that spring.

At last, the other companies—including McCormick's—had to admit defeat and come to Johnnie and buy the rights to make twine-binding harvesters. By 1888, more than ninety percent of all the grain harvested in the United States depended on the twine binder, a process that began with "Johnnie's knot."

Today, John Francis Appleby is mainly forgotten. Try looking him up in your favorite encyclopedia. But in that era he became a hero. Cyrus McCormick, Jr., called Johnnie "one of the great names in the history of American invention." And in the opinion of one engineering expert, the Appleby twine binder was "the crowning achievement of mechanics—the most ingenious invention of the nineteenth century."

# AL GLOVER
## CRASH COURSE

For Al Glover, a farm boy who grew up near Lacey's Cross-Road, Alabama, it all started with model airplanes. The year was 1945, the fourth year of America's involvement in World War II, and partly due to the boom in war-related jobs, the Great Depression in this country had neared its end. But not in rural Alabama, where many families still lived in poverty and struggled to make ends meet.

Al had numerous jobs on the family farm: plowing, picking cotton, stripping cornstalks for livestock feed, and weeding the garden. In addition, his father ran a small shingle factory, and the boy helped heat the water that softened the wood used for shingles. These were all tedious physical jobs that gave him time to think, and his thoughts often turned to inventions.

A few years later, Al would come up with the idea for rear-window defrosters for cars. "A guy had a Kaiser [a car from that era] and one winter morning the guy was warming up his car and the ice on all the windows melted but the rear. I thought, Man, you should run an electric wire back there." But, as Al notes ruefully, "I didn't have the know-how."

When he was seventeen and TV was sweeping the country, he would conceive of a switch that would automatically mute the TV sound as the viewer picked up the telephone. Again, he didn't have any means to follow up his inspiration.

But in 1945, when he was thirteen, Al had one idea he was able to go with nearly all the way. At the time, his love was aviation. Earning extra money by selling newspapers, he bought and flew model airplanes built from balsa-wood kits. The vehicles ran on tiny gas engines and were flown on hand-held tether lines.

Al and his friends spent many hours with their planes. Nowadays, model planes that fly are usually radio-controlled, but then the planes were flown round and round in circles on fish line or piano wire. The model always strained at the limit of the line, like a dog pulling on a leash, and if the line didn't stay taut, the plane went out of control and crashed.

Another tricky maneuver was changing vertical direction. The tether lines could make the plane climb or dive by moving the flaps on the rear or trailing-edge of the wings and the elevator on the tail. But to change from a dive into a climb was risky. "You needed a long sweeping turn rather than an abrupt change," says Al. All too often, the vehicles couldn't pull out of their sharp descents and they crashed.

Al and his friends would retrieve the tiny motors and insert them into new plane bodies. But as they accumulated a sort of boneyard of balsa parts, Al began to remake the plane bodies. One step led to another, and soon Al was trying out his own ideas for airplane bodies. His friend Tommy Whitehead recalls that in those days Al "would come up with . . . just weird designs that flew well, he just drew the planes outta his head."

Al decided there had to be a way to prevent the crashes, something to help pull the planes out of nosedives. His idea was a wing modification, a device he called a drooped leading-edge flap.

It was a strange moment in the history of invention. During the same period, unknown to Al, aerodynamic engineers across the ocean, in Germany, were working on a similar idea. Using wind tunnels and shops operated by some of the foremost machinists in the world, these technologists had adopted leading-edge wing modifications for Hitler's Air Force. The actual invention first occurred to a German World War I pilot named Lachmann, who thought of it while recuperating in the hospital from a crash caused when his fighter plane stalled. After World War I, he tried to patent his idea but was rejected by the German patent office. About the same time, a British inventor, Handley Page, hit on the same invention independently, received a British patent, and then, upon hearing of Lachmann's work, brought the German to England to work for his company. Curiously, despite the efforts of Handley Page and Dr. Lachmann, their invention found relatively few users in Britain. At the onset of World War II, however, German aerodynamic specialists were taking advantage of the device.

Enter Al. That a thirteen-year-old American kid improvising on model-plane parts, with only a self-taught knowledge of aerodynamics, with no encouragement (Al's strict father actually disapproved of his hobby), was experimenting with the same idea as Hitler's engineers is mind-boggling.

A leading-edge wing flap provides the same function as the trailing-edge wing flap—it increases available lift, the aerodynamic force that moves a plane vertically. How do you assemble the device? Al explains: "Make the wing have a seam one-third of the way back, a separate piece like the flap. When the back flaps go down, this also goes down. It gives more lift."

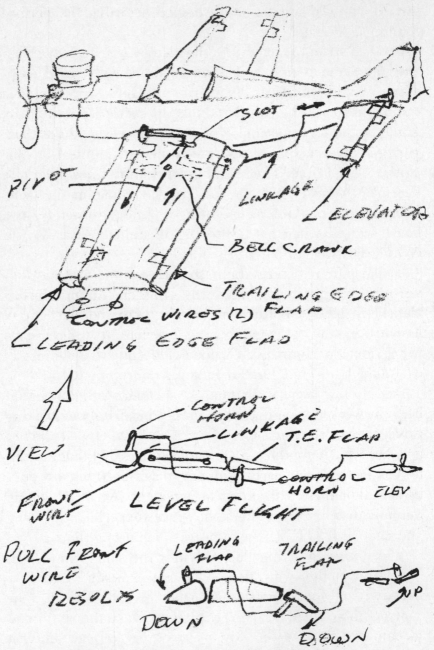

*Al Glover's sketch of his leading-edge innova-tion*

In Europe, this innovation helped improve the performance of German Messerschmitt 109 fighter planes and others. In Alabama, it was helping a kid and his friends fly their model planes better. "I tried it and it worked," Al says simply.

Al didn't think about marketing his invention until the 1950s, when he was working as a draftsman and designer with various technical companies in the Huntsville, Alabama, area. He wanted to develop his own projects off-hours in the family garage and decided to patent the wing design from his childhood. But after doing some research, he discovered that he had been preceded. And that was the end of the project.

As an adult, Al went on to great success at Chrysler, where he won more patents than any other designer during the 1980s. Many of these designs are very much part of our lives today: they are fuel-efficiency devices and speedometer gadgets and sensors hidden behind the panels of our cars.

How did a rural kid who never earned a college degree became a leading-edge inventor? Perhaps his relaxed approach helped. Just as playing around with a favorite hobby got Al inventing as a child, something close to that started him as an adult. He began inventing for his employers during his lunch hours. "I just did it for the fun of it," he remembers. "Invention lets you express yourself."

# Tom Blanchard
## A STUTTERING START

**A**s a kid, Thomas Blanchard had problems.

He was born into a large family on June 24, 1788, near Worcester, Massachusetts, and grew up in farming country. His earliest memories were of "cutting up shingles with a knife into all kinds of toys, such as windmills and waterwheels." Miles from cities and specialized urban workshops, he lived in a world of plowboys, not highly trained mechanics and craftsmen. As a friend put it, "Thomas was wholly misplaced."

He had another problem, too—he stuttered. The farmers in the nearby potato fields burdened him with the nickname "Stammering Tom." His speech impediment brought him trouble in the classroom: when he stood up to recite his lessons (memorizing and reciting were standard procedure in schools then), sometimes he just couldn't get the words out. The local schoolmaster labeled him a "dullard."

Finally, Tom left school, and his family went through a difficult period trying to determine where he would fit in. According to one neighbor:

*When Thomas was about twelve years of age his father came to my father and asked him to take the boy into his employ as he could do nothing with him. He would not work, but was constantly at some project in the line of machinery. Thomas soon became a source of trial and vexation and did not remain long. If father sent him into the field to pick and pile up stones Tom would stammer out "T-t-there might b-b-be a ma-machine m-m-made to do th-th-this!"*

Although he'd always tinkered with devices carved from wood, Tom only hit on his first real invention when he was thirteen years old, after a friend mentioned to him that someone in Boston had invented an apple-paring machine.

Intrigued by the idea, Tom set out to make his own version of the machine, with no model to go by. What pushed him may have been a tongue-tied boy's wish to make a splash at a "bee."

Bees were parties that combined work with play, common in pre-Civil War America. Some were quilting bees, for the ladies, and some were shingle bees, during which the men would help repair barns. Kids especially enjoyed apple bees, where they peeled apples as the first stage in making applesauce. The apple bees drew crowds of young people from the community to skin the apple harvest. They would divide into teams to see who could work the fastest; sometimes individual workers would challenge each other to one-on-one contests.

After a week of experimenting, Tom completed his first apple-paring machine. The apparatus consisted of a spindle that, inserted through the apple's core, turned with a crank so that the surface of the apple would move over a knife blade. Unfortunately, when he tried it out for the first time, the knife sank into the core of the fruit before it finished removing the skin.

Tom didn't give up. Before trying to perfect his machine, he carefully observed someone paring an apple, noticing how the thumb in the cutting hand guided the blade itself. When he returned to his invention, he welded to the blade a heavy wire that worked like a thumb. This improvement made it possible for the new device to do just what he wanted. The next time he went to an apple bee, Tom could peel apples faster than six opponents combined.

Word of the device spread to other farms. Tom must have taken pride in having invented something that worked, but he had another reason for satisfaction: instead of being thought of as a vexatious dullard, weird in his ways, he got some applause for being an inventive kid. In a later biographical interview, Blanchard remembered that, because of this gadget, he "became a favorite at all the paring bees."

Although Tom continued to tinker, his second successful machine didn't appear until 1806, when he was eighteen. It was this invention—another labor-saving device—that started his professional career. His father had sent him to work in his older brother's tack factory in the nearby town of West Millbury. At the time, tacks (not modern thumbtacks, but small, sharp-pointed nails with a broad flat head) were made by hand by semi-skilled workers. As Tom labored at this slow and tiresome job, hammering one end of each tack into a flat head one at a time in a vise, he wondered if he could come up with a tack machine. His brother Stephen said this was impossible, but that didn't stop Tom. The machine became his "darling project."

Within less than a year, he had devised a working model that turned out tacks, according to one observer, "as fast as the ticks of a clock." It was a machine consisting of knives and hammers run by gears and wheels on a centrally powered spindle. In essence, the same device is used to make tacks to this very day. First, metal sheets of the needed width and thickness are fed into the apparatus. These sheets are then cut into wedge-shaped strips by two knives known as "jaws," with each wedge destined to be a tack. The tip of the wedge will be the point of the tack. One knife, or side of the jaw, withdraws, while the other jaw holds the strip with the aid of a metal finger and brings it against a steel block, called a "die," which holds sheet metal to be stamped. Next, a hammer pounds the thicker end of the wedge, creating the tack head. As soon as the hammer recedes and the die blocks part, a metal arm driven by the spindle pushes out the completed tack.

Tom didn't patent his first working model. For nearly five years, he tinkered and improved and refined the machine, so that when he finally applied for a patent, his contraption was much more accurate than his original, and faster, too—it produced five hundred tacks a minute. On October 3, 1817, as soon as he was awarded the patent, he turned around and sold the rights for $5,000. In that era, $5,000 was enough for Tom to marry, buy a house, and go into business as a professional inventor.

Two years later, Tom had his biggest invention come to him "in a flash." It was an improvement on the lathe, a machine that shapes an object by holding and turning it against the edge of a cutting tool.

In 1819, a lathe could cut only one shape. If you put a block of wood on the spindle and turned it against the cutter, the result might be a broom handle or a table leg, but it would always be round. Irregular shapes, such as that of a rifle stock, could be produced only by laborious hand-carving.

To address this shortcoming, Tom conceived of a strip of metal, which we now call a "cam," which connected the cutting blade to a rolling ball or wheel. This ball or wheel would roll over the shape to be copied, and transmit the shape to the movements of the cutting blade.

*Drawing of Tom Blanchard's improved lathe, rigged to make shoe lasts*

Tom's improved lathe introduced a level of accuracy pre-viously unknown in that era of handmade products. Tasks such as making shoe lasts (the foot-shaped forms over which shoes are made or repaired) that had taken days when done by hand could now be tossed off in a matter of minutes. More important, whereas handmade parts weren't precisely uniform, parts made on a Blanchard lathe were so alike they could be removed from one machine and func-tion in another. This interchangeability helped make mass production possible, and is a concept essential to all mod-ern-day manufacturing.

Tom developed his lathe while working for a manufac-turer of rifles for the U.S. Army. Until the Patent Act of 1836, the term of patents was only fourteen years. When his patent expired in 1834, Tom argued that his work for the government had prevented him from earning a full profit from his invention. As a result, Congress granted him an extension.

In 1848, when his lathe patent expired again, Tom asked that Congress extend it for a second time. The inventor claimed he had been so overwhelmed by legal costs, de-fending his rights in court against patent violators, that he had still not profited from his valuable contribution. As part of his case, Tom invited legislative leaders to the ro-tunda of the Capitol. Henry Clay, Daniel Webster, John Calhoun, and others arrived to discover busts of them-selves copied in marble. Using plaster statues as a guide, Tom had quickly and efficiently carved the copies in stone using his lathes, duplicating every delicate stroke of the original artwork. The lawmakers were convinced, and Congress granted Tom the extension. A lawyer who op-posed the bill said, "Tom Blanchard has 'turned the heads' of Congress."

Tom was often called upon to defend his patent rights in

court, sometimes pleading his case before senators and representatives. He did such a good job that demand grew for him as a speaker and consultant. His confidence increased, and his stuttering went away, never to reappear.

Very few people know Thomas Blanchard's name today. Although his lathe is not as noticeable a part of day-to-day life as the light bulb or the auto or the airplane, it is just as important to the way we live. Almost all manufactured goods depend, directly or indirectly, on processes in which a lathe is accurately guided by a pattern.

As one nineteenth-century patent expert noted, "Among the great inventions of the day, Tom Blanchard's hold their place, for the most part unobscured and unimproved."

# BECKY SCHROEDER
## ENLIGHTENED THINKER

Rebecca Schroeder entered the world of invention at the age of ten, while a pupil at Ladyfield Academy in Toledo, Ohio. One October evening, she had gone with her mother to a shopping center and was waiting in the car, poring over her studies, while her mother hurried in for some groceries.

"I was in the car doing my homework when it started to get dark," she told reporters later. "I kept thinking what a good thing it would be if people could write in the dark."

Her father encouraged her to pursue her inspirations. "I'm always coming up with ideas," explained Becky when the media thronged around her. "It happens when you least expect it."

At first, she kept the idea to herself. The homework arrived on the teacher's desk the next day, but the idea of writing in the dark glimmered in her mind for many days, until she went to the library to find out what kinds of things glow in the dark.

"Fluorescence" was the word she had in mind. Wrong—fluorescent compounds fade just after they're removed from the light. Next she considered "bioluminescence," meaning the emission of light by organisms. Glowworms? Fireflies? Would some living creature light her inspiration? When that didn't seem promising, Becky discovered "phosphorescence," the action of certain substances that produce a glow after exposure to light.

At first, she thought of an ink that would glow in the dark, but then she had another idea: what about coating the surface of something like a clipboard with phosphorescent material? Then, if she set writing paper on top, the board would glow through, silhouetting any letters on the paper, thereby making them visible in the dark.

Charles Schroeder describes it this way: "She came home. She said, 'I have an invention.' I said, 'Oh.' Then her mother said, 'I think she really does.'"

The next step? A trip to a hobby shop to get phosphorescent paint. Then she needed a room with no windows, so she commandeered one of the family's bathrooms for her laboratory. And one evening, after her first experiments, Becky Schroeder ran into the family room, shouting, "Come see! It works!"

Charles Schroeder was impressed. "The thing worked better than I thought it could have worked," he says. In the blackness, his daughter held up a glowing rectangle on which he could read her message: "I can write in the dark."

Two years later, on August 27, 1974, the U.S. Patent and Trademark Office awarded Becky patent #3,832,556 for a "Luminescent Backing Sheet for Writing in the Dark." Newspapers and magazines rushed to tell her story; she appeared on a number of television shows and won several awards.

In the years that followed, Becky has been granted almost a dozen patents that stake out improvements on her basic idea. Becky formed a company called BJ Products (BJ stands for Becky Jane), and now she calls her product Glo-Sheet.

Who are the potential customers for Glo-Sheet? At various times, both the U.S. Navy and NASA have taken a serious look at the invention. Becky sees many uses for it, for people such as pilots in darkened cockpits; policemen filling

*From Becky Schroeder's patent: "A tablet of writing paper (14) having a top sheet (12) lifted and turned back for insertion of a phosphorescent backing sheet (10) of my invention"*

out forms and soldiers in war zones at night; doctors, nurses, and other medical personnel making their evening rounds; and movie and theater critics who need to jot notes during shows. But to date, although many Glo-Sheets have been sold directly, Becky has found no distributor.

For her brainstorm, Becky was named an Ohio Inventor of the Year, and was inducted into the Ohio Inventors Hall of Fame. Today, more than twenty years later, she is in demand to speak about invention at state and national meetings, and at schools and universities. Now married, she assists her husband in running his own insurance agency, and she also uses her creativity in designing jewelry for a local store.

To kids, her message is: "Childhood? That's where you start inventing." And she warns them against listening to naysayers, those people, sometimes friends or family, who may unconsciously discourage kid inventors because they themselves do not believe. Becky says, "Keep an open mind—things could come up."

Today, when people hear about Glo-Sheet, they are still intrigued. Kids get excited about writing letters at summer camp after lights-out, for example—or other everyday applications. And they like Becky's story, too, the story of a little girl who conquered the dark with a bright idea.

# ELIHU THOMSON
## THE SHOCKER

Some veteran inventors look back with pride at their first invention. This is true of Elihu Thomson, who by the end of his life held nearly seven hundred patents, even though to some his early childhood inventions must seem a little embarrassing.

It was the winter of 1864, and Elihu lived in a part of Philadelphia known as "The Neck," a neighborhood of tiny row houses jammed with recent immigrants to the United States. His Scottish working-class parents had come to this country when he was only five.

One December evening, the schoolmaster knocked on the Thomsons' door. He had to discuss a problem involving Elihu. The problem had nothing to do with street gangs, even though Elihu belonged to the Moyamensings, a gang which took its name from Moyamensing Prison, a few blocks down the street. The problem, explained the young teacher, was that Elihu had done so well.

Somehow, in his rough-and-tumble world, Elihu had managed to become an excellent student. He had sped through his studies, mastering all the subjects his grammar school taught. His teachers believed he could go on to success at the famous Central High School in Philadelphia. But because Elihu wasn't yet the required thirteen years of age, he had to wait a year before enrolling. What to do until then? the teacher asked.

The Thomsons did not decide on the spot. They considered Elihu's future very carefully. The school had recommended a year of physical exercise to build up the slender boy's strength. But Elihu proposed another scheme—he would use the time to pursue home study in science and invention.

Mary Thomson, Elihu's mother, believed in the value of a scientific education. When her son was five years old, she had made a point of showing him the famous Donati's comet streaking across the Philadelphia skies in the summer of 1858. This sparked an interest in astronomy that would last the rest of Elihu's life. And Daniel, his father, perhaps encouraged Elihu to study his back issues of *The Imperial Journal of Art, Science, Mechanics, and Engineering.* Did not the study of science, as the magazine's editors claimed, influence "the formation of moral and intellectual character"? At first, the answer for Elihu was no.

He still belonged to the Moyamensings, and the gang members depended on the kid they nicknamed "Lihu" for great ideas for new weapons. Early in his independent study, Elihu had devised a very effective blowgun that spat out bits of raw potato shaped like bullets. Then there was an even more advanced weapon, the "sucker."

Daniel Thomson, whose job often took him away on business trips, came home to rumors of his son's latest innovation. But what, the father wanted to know, was a "sucker"?

Elihu explained that in gang fights the boys pried loose cobblestones from the streets to hurl at the enemy. Sometimes they spent more time prying stones loose than actually throwing them. Elihu's device, the "sucker," was a leather contraption that popped the stones out quickly.

Daniel Thomson was not happy. And Elihu remembered forever the stern question his father asked him: "Why don't you try *real* experiments?"

Elihu accepted the challenge. First, he decided to experiment in photography, which in those days was itself a field of discovery. Chemists were finding new and better photochemical processes to create pictures. But how could Elihu enter this pioneering field? There were no how-to manuals. Hoping to encourage his enthusiasm, his mother purchased a volume, *The Magician's Own Book*, which contained a section on optics. Photography was not mentioned, but when Elihu paged to the middle of the book, he discovered many household experiments using electricity.

These pages in *The Magician's Own Book* led to Elihu's first electric experiment. Following their lead, Elihu put together a machine that created static electricity. It was a device that attached a wine bottle to a spindle. By rubbing the glass of the bottle against a strip of silk, Elihu could make enough electricity to discharge a spark. He could store the charge, too. The book also showed him how to make a Leyden jar, a device that had been around for more than a century, consisting of a glass jar coated with metal foil on the inside and outside, with a metal conductor going through a stoppered lid to the foil inside.

When Daniel Thomson returned from his next business trip, he mocked his son's efforts. To Daniel, these homespun machines must have seemed as juvenile as the "sucker." Sure, electricity was a science. But the elder Thomson thought it would never amount to more than a novelty, a trifle, a gimmick.

Elihu protested that the machine could produce a shock and asked his father to touch the Leyden jar. Daniel Thomson did. He laughed. "You call that pinprick a shock?"

In the days that followed, Elihu tried to make a more potent machine, using *The Magician's Own Book* as a guide. Clearly, his little Leyden jar didn't store enough energy. But what if he connected a series of jars? The result would be a primitive battery.

### HOW TO MAKE AN ELECTRICAL MACHINE.

It is very easy to make a glass machine of the cylindrical form, if the maker cannot afford to buy one. First procure

a common wine bottle of good dimensions, and thickish glass. Drill a hole through its bottom, by igniting a piece of worsted tied round round it, dipped in turpentine, which will do this. Through this hole and the mouth pass a spindle, as represented in the cut. The end of B should be squared to

fix a handle on, and the spindle should be fixed firmly in the bottle. The bottle is then to be fixed in a frame, in the following manner: The end of the spindle c passes through a hole at B; and the other end at c has the handle for turning the machine.

Next make a cushion of wash-leather, stuffed with wool, and fastened to the top of a frame of the following figure.

CUSHION.

This frame is to be of such a height that the cushion shall press against the sides of the bottle, and a piece of black silk is sewn on to the top of the cushion, and hangs over the bottle D. The cushion should be smeared with an amalgam, formed by melting together in the bowl of a tobacco pipe, one part of tin with two of zinc; to which, while fluid, should be added six parts of mercury. These should be stirred about till quite cold, and then reduced to a fine powder in a mortar, and mixed with a sufficient quantity of lard to form a thickish paste When all is done, the machine is complete.

### CONDUCTOR.

The electricity being generated by the friction produced between the rubber and the bottle from the motion imparted by the handle, it is necessary to draw it off for use. This is performed by what is called a conductor. This is made in the following manner: At right angles to one end of a cylinder of wood, about two inches and a half in diameter, and six inches long, fix a small wooden cylinder about three quarters of an inch in diameter, and three inches long, rounded at both ends—the other end of the larger cylinder is also to be rounded. Cover the whole with tinfoil, and mount it on a stand on a glass rod. When used, it is to be placed with the even piece in a line even with, and about half an inch from the bottle, and it should be of such a height as to come just below the silk apron. When it is wished to charge a Leyden jar it is to be placed at the round end of the conductor.

### HOW TO GET A JAR FULL OF ELECTRICITY.

A most useful piece of electrical apparatus is called the Leyden jar, here represented. It is employed for the purpose of obtaining a quantity of electricity, which may be applied to any substance. It consists of a glass jar, coated

both inside and without, four fifths of the way up, with tinfoil. A knob rises through a wooden top, communicating with the inside of the jar. When it is wished to charge the jar, this knob is applied to the prime conductor of the electrical machine when in action, and a quantity of electricity being given off, the jar will remain charged with it till a connection is made, by some good conductor of electricity, between the knob and the outside tinfoil. A piece of brass chain must hang from the stem that carries the knob, and connect it with the interior of the ja

### THE ELECTRICAL BATTERY.

If several of these jars be united, an enormous quantity of electricity can be collected; but in arranging them, all the interior coatings must be made to communicate by me tallic rods, and a similar union must be effected among the exterior coatings. When thus arranged, the whole series may be charged as if they formed but one jar.

For the purpose of making a direct communication between the inner or outer coatings of a jar or battery, by which a discharge is effected, an instrument called a discharging rod is employed. It consists of two bent metallic rods, terminating at one end by brass balls, and connected at another by a joint which is fixed to the end of a glass handle, and which, acting like a pair of compasses, allows of the balls being separated at certain distances. When opened to the proper degree, one of the balls is made to touch the exterior coating, and the other ball is then brought into contact with the knob of the jar, when a discharge is effected; while the glass handle secures the person holding it from the effects of the shock.

*From* The Magician's Own Book

He put some water in each jar and immersed them in water and connected them all in a row to his friction machine. Choosing a cold evening, when static electricity is most easily generated, he cranked his wine-bottle machine hundreds of times. Then Elihu invited his father to repeat the experiment.

This time, when Mr. Thomson touched the top of the jar, it hissed and the shock flung him onto his back. Thomson was stunned and his wife had to run in from the next room to help him to his feet. The frightened boy had had no idea his device would deliver such power. He told his father how sorry he was and waited for his punishment. But there was no punishment.

Daniel Thomson stared at the machine thoughtfully, grinned, and promised never again to laugh at Elihu's inventions. Here, as he painfully knew, was an experiment that was *real*.

As an adult, Elihu Thomson combined the careers of scientist, inventor, and teacher. Many of his inventions founded whole industries. Elihu first devised the breakthrough process of electric welding, the technology which is necessary to make autos, boats, building frames, and many other heavy-duty products and even the small incandescent filaments used in electronics tubes. His magnetic blow-out device gave birth to the automatic circuit breaker, the mechanism in homes and businesses which protects electrical circuits from overloading. In addition, he invented improved dynamos, an electric meter, devices that made consumer use of alternating current a reality, an electric air drill, and the repulsion induction motor, whose principle still operates in today's vacuum cleaners. After the Battle of the Currents was resolved, the electric company based on Elihu's inventions merged with the Edison General Electric Company to form GE, the modern corporate giant.

As an adult, Elihu stayed away from the public spotlight, turning down directorships on companies his inventions had created. He was famous among other experimenters for the kindness with which he gave them advice and help. When Thomson died on March 13, 1937, at the age of eighty-three, American scientists and inventors mourned his passing.

# MATTIE KNIGHT
## FORGOTTEN GIRL

Nineteenth-century America had a love affair with invention. Everyone got into the act. The young, the old, the rich, the poor, they all seemed spurred by the drive to invent. Mark Twain took credit for several inventions and patented them, including a self-pasting scrapbook that made a small profit. More surprising is Henry David Thoreau, the man who wrote the famous book *Walden* about wanting to retreat from the hubbub of society and live simply with Nature: he devoted more than a year to inventing a manufacturing process that would mass-produce the perfect pencil. Even a future President invented—Abe Lincoln received a patent for a device for lifting riverboats over shoals in 1849, and during the Civil War he took occasional breaks from work to examine new military inventions in a vacant lot near the White House.

Boy inventors made news, too. When the British Parliament noticed the explosion of patents from the new republic, they sent a committee to investigate. Their conclusion? "There is not a working boy of average ability in the New England States who has not an idea of some mechanical invention." A famous poem of that era highlights a boy inventor named Darius Green, who tries to invent a flying machine. Reports on a real boy inventor, Tom Blanchard, quoted charming stories from his childhood neighbors.

But as far as female inventors are concerned, there is much less information; and about girl inventors, almost nothing.

Some fashion historians report that in 1798 twelve-year-old Betsey Metcalf of Providence, Rhode Island, invented the straw bonnet. She didn't exactly—most likely, the straw bonnet was invented in Italy, but when shipments of Italian bonnets didn't arrive on these shores, she used American materials to create an American version. There are many more details we would like to know, beyond what has survived. What kind of thinker was this resourceful person and what are the various stages in her story?

Or the gimlet-screw girl? Early screws could not make the hole into which they were sunk—first you had to drill a hole and then insert the screw. The gimlet-pointed screw created its own hole while you inserted it. A respected writer, H. J. Mozans (a pseudonym for a feminist priest named John Augustine Zahm), mentions in *Woman in Science* that "the gimlet-pointed screw, which was the idea of a little girl, has realized to its patentee an independent fortune." Who *was* this girl? When and where did she do it? There is evidence she may have been Harriet Brisbane of Charleston, South Carolina, who later received seventeen patents as an adult inventor under her married name, Harriet Tracy. But no one seems to have preserved information about Harriet and she remains a mystery figure.

And what about Beatrice Kenner, now honored as the African American female inventor with the most patents? When she was a six year old in Charlotte, North Carolina, in 1919, she tried to invent a self-oiling hinge to silence a door that squeaked her awake every morning. Unfortunately, the details are lost.

If kids in previous eras were to be seen and not heard, it seems that American girl inventors were to be briefly noticed and underreported. What more could be expected in an age that denied women the vote? But one nineteenth-century girl inventor we do know something about is Mattie Knight.

When she died at the age of seventy-five in 1914, one newspaper hailed her as a "woman Edison." Her laboratory at 110 High Street in Boston had become a landmark.

Motors were her love, and this talented and determined inventor seems to have devised all types, from steam and hot-air engines to gas turbos and gas rotary motors. Her own firsthand experience as a worker in textile factories led her to design manufacturing machines. Mattie came up with at least six advances in heavy machinery used by shoe manufacturers. Her ingenuity also resulted in new designs for windows, a dress and skirt shield, an advance in tin-can manufacturing, a "silent" automobile motor, and even a clasp meant to hold a woman's robe.

By the time of her death, Mattie had become a beloved figure, known for her bravery in defending the rights to her ideas. In obituaries, newspapers stated that she had received eighty-seven patents. Actually, she received twenty-seven patents, but her contributions are very real, as real as the paper bags grocery shoppers carry to the car from the supermarket. In 1867, when she was twenty-nine, Mattie devised an improvement to a paper-feeding machine which to this day is used to produce square-bottomed paper grocery sacks.

What about Mattie the kid inventor? We have a few glimmers. Born in 1838, she was raised in Maine and New Hampshire, and she and her brothers and sisters labored in textile mills at an early age. "I have from my earliest recollection been connected in some way with machinery," re-

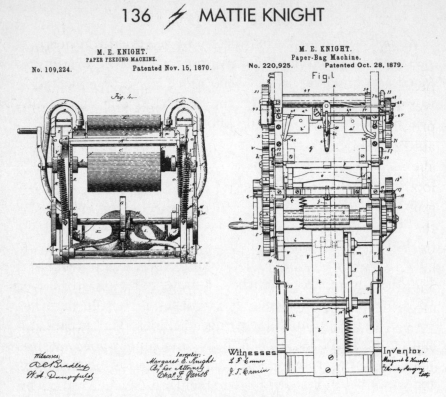

M. E. KNIGHT.
PAPER FEEDING MACHINE.
No. 109,224.       Patented Nov. 15, 1870.

M. E. KNIGHT.
Paper-Bag Machine.
No. 220,925.    Patented Oct. 28, 1879.

*From two of Mattie Knight's patents*

called Mattie in a patent-interference suit. And in a letter to a friend she described her early leanings:

*As a child, I never cared for the things that girls usually do . . . the only things I wanted were a jackknife, a gimlet [a nineteenth-century hand-powered drill], and pieces of wood . . . I sighed sometimes because I was not like other girls, but wisely concluded that I couldn't help it, and sought further consolation from my tools. I was always making things for my brothers. Did they want anything in the line of playthings, they always said, "Mattie will make them for us."*

With time, her projects grew bigger. She was famous for her kites, and her sleds were "the envy and admiration" of every boy in town.

When she was twelve years old, Margaret Knight visited the textile mill where her brothers worked. There she witnessed an accident in which someone was injured, and she went home and got to thinking. The New Hampshire mill produced cotton cloth. The cotton strands sped through an automated loom, and if the strands snarled, the steel-tipped shuttles could fall out. Shuttles are devices used in the looms for passing the thread of the woof—the threads going crosswise—back and forth between the threads of the warp—the threads going lengthwise. If a falling shuttle hit a worker, it could cause serious injury. Mattie's solution was a stop-motion device that shut everything down when the strands went awry. The grateful mill owners immediately put her safety device into use.

As an adult, Mattie came up with many other valuable inventions, some patented and others sold outright to her employers. But as she later looked back on her inventions, Mattie remembered the happiest moment in her career as the time she came up with a safety device when she was only twelve years old.

# EPILOGUE
## ADVICE FOR YOUNG INVENTORS

What if you come up with an idea for a great invention? How do you protect your idea? How do you claim it as your own? How do you bring it to the marketplace?

There are several steps you can take.

The first and most important is to keep records of the development of your invention. Use a journal to keep track of your ideas and experiments. Be sure to include the time, date, and location in your notes. When your device works, give a demonstration of the invention to trustworthy witnesses, including an adult. Unfortunately, if your claim ever goes to court, witnesses who are relatives will not carry much weight. You should resort to a trustworthy nonrelative to witness your brainstorm. Have them sign and date a statement about what they saw.

Next comes the patent search. The basic question here is whether your brainstorm is new. Professional patent searchers are available, but costs for an average search range from $500 to $1,500. You can do some preliminary searching on your own. First, look online and in retail stores that specialize in similar products. Do some Googling. Order catalogues from firms in your specialty and look them over. If you discover a product like yours, you haven't lost months of allowance money paying somebody else to find out, and in the process, you've learned more about a field in which you've already had one inspiration. Maybe this experience will joggle loose another great idea.

If your device isn't in the marketplace, the next stage is to search the Patent Office files. You can go online to search at the United States Patent and Trademark Office Web site (www.uspto.gov/patft/index.html). You don't have to be a professional to do some very effective searching here, and there are no charges. The Patent Office offers excellent help at its Kids' Pages (www.uspto.gov/go/kids). Click the link "The Imagination Machine," then the link "We dare you . . . to be a Patent Detective." You will find clear instructions on how to patent search. A relatively simple search might take about four hours. One disadvantage of this Web site is that the images are tiff files and may prove difficult to access and print. Should you feel uncertain about your results, you can still consult one of the Patent Depository Libraries that the federal government has established at public and university libraries around the country; these are staffed by librarians who are patent specialists—they are sources of good advice. Some branches are so busy, however, that you may need to call in advance to make an appointment.

It is good news if nothing shows up in your search, but you are not yet done. Inventions patented before 1976 do not appear in the searchable database. The patents, of course, go back to 1790, but earlier ones are accessible only by issue date, patent number, and current U.S. classification. For many patent searchers, the remarkable Google Patent Search (www.google.com/patents) is the preferred online tool—it is straightforward, easy to use, and can search the full text of older patents (the U.S. Patent Office site does not have this feature). Another commercial site with a good reputation is Free Patents Online (www.freepatentsonline. com). Millions of other patents filed are filed abroad with other governments. Check out the European Patent Office (http://ep.espacenet.com). It allows searching of multiple worldwide patent databases at once and has pdf files available for those patents. The service is free. You may also do some searching of American patents at this site.

If research continues to indicate that your idea is unique, it may be time to take the big step of seeking adult specialist help. You will need a patent attorney or patent agent. These specialists have been awarded licenses to practice before the U.S. Patent and Trademark Office, a status earned by passing a rigorous exam. Either an agent or an attorney can help you apply for a patent—the difference is that attorneys have legal expertise and knowledge of courts and contracts; agents typically have a technical background and may have special knowledge about the field of your brainstorm. You will find a list of these people and their contact information at the Patent Office Web site. When you choose someone, be cautious. If you ask a local inventors' club or association, they may be able to recommend agents and lawyers their members have found reliable and honest. Keep in mind that fees are high, and that there is a fee for filing a patent application and for getting a patent issued. At some point it's sensible to do an analysis of potential costs versus benefits—does your invention seem likely to produce enough sales to recover the cost of seeking a patent?

Other services which may help kid inventors include: state government programs to encourage patent applications (some states offer free search services); the regional offices of the U.S. Small Business Administration (a solo inventor is a very small business); university centers that offer help to entrepreneurs; the many regional inventors' clubs and associations which have sprung up in recent years; and various city, state, and federal programs that target special groups like African Americans, Hispanics, women, and others for help in starting up enterprises.

Another breakthrough for your invention might result from an inventor competition. The advantage here is instant publicity for your product if you win. There are a host of well-known contests for kids as well as adults, and a fascinating number of kids' contests now specialize in the invention of games and toys. Reality-show invention contests open to adults as well as children have hit the airwaves, but scrutinize the conditions for entering them very carefully. One of the most famous requires that contestants sign over control of the invention to the show's producers and offers the inventor 35 percent of future profits. Is that a good deal, or not? You will need to think it through cautiously.

In addition, be wary of television and magazine ads that promise fame and fortune to inventors. Most registered agents and attorneys do not market themselves this way. Beware of promises of big money, leather-bound portfolios analyzing your prospects for success, and demands for big money up front (reputable agents and lawyers do not work this way, although a few may demand a relatively modest retainer). To find out more about how to avoid the scammers, see this brochure produced by the Patent and Trademark office: www.uspto.gov/web/offices/com/iip/documents/scamprevent.pdf.

If at last you apply for a patent, keep in mind that the Patent Office frequently takes several years to decide whether to grant a patent. However, just filing a patent application gives an invention some protection and often inventors begin marketing their brainstorm after taking this big step. A patent lawyer can advise you about this.

There is another alternative. Don't patent your invention at all.

Some inventions are simply not patentable, no matter how valuable they may be. Cathy Evans, Ralph Samuelson, and Hannah Cannon were all inventors in these circumstances. Some inventors seek patents for the ego boost involved (specialists call these "vanity patents"), but most inventors wish to fill a real need and be rewarded for it. One Georgia boy inventor, whose story is not covered in these pages, came up with a device that he sold door-to-door, often making in one afternoon what adult wage earners brought home for a week. He never patented it. Perhaps his idea, a simple one that could easily have been stolen, was ideal for his approach: he devoted his time and energies to selling the thing.

Another alternative may seem startling at first, but it has worked for some inventors. The approach is simply to *wait*. Philo Farnsworth, Frank Epperson, Johnnie Appleby, and Jerrald Spencer all waited until they were adults to develop their inventions. Obviously, this can be risky. Will your brainstorm remain undiscovered that long? Or is someone else at this very moment developing the same product? No one can know in advance.

If you finally get the patent, then you're in business, and the next step is to market the product. May good fortune be yours.

But if you're unable to get a patent, it's not the end of the road. As the chapters in this book show, sometimes an invention is merely one moment in the process of creative thought. Al Glover, Mary Spaeth, Tom Edison, and Robert Goddard didn't get their childhood inspirations patented either, but went on to success as adult inventors. Perhaps you can follow in their footsteps.

# GLOSSARY

**COPYRIGHT:** Legal protection for authors and artists which gives them the exclusive right to publish or sell their works and determine who else can publish them

**INTERFERENCE:** A proceeding in the U.S. Patent and Trademark Office, initiated when more than one inventor claims the same invention, to determine who should be awarded the patent

**LICENSING:** The process by which an inventor sells to someone else the right to produce and market an invention within a certain territory. In exchange, the inventor often receives royalty payments

**OUTRIGHT SALE:** The sale by an inventor of all rights and responsibilities in connection with an invention to another party

**PATENT:** A contract between the government and an inventor that gives the inventor the exclusive right to make, use, or sell an invention in the United States for a period of twenty years from the date the patent application is filed, in exchange for public disclosure of the details of the invention

**PROTOTYPE:** The original working model of an invention

**ROYALTIES:** Payments by a licensee of an invention to the inventor for each article sold under a patent license

**TRADEMARK:** A brand name or symbol that specifies that a product is made by a particular company, to distinguish it from goods made by others

# Sources

CHESTER GREENWOOD: Interviews with Jacqueline Chandler, George Greenwood, and Cathryn Wilson (of the Maine State Library); Steven Caney, *Steven Caney's Invention Book*, 1985; Sid Moody, "Earmuffs," *Chicago Tribune*, Feb. 16, 1988; Leonard Zehr, "Chester's Cold Ears," *Wall Street Journal*, Feb. 10, 1986; unpublished Greenwood family papers from the Maine State Library.

VANESSA HESS: Interviews with Vanessa Hess, Dan Huffman, and Maurine Marchani; "Young Inventor Helps Disabled Friend Write," *Current Science*, Nov. 17, 1989.

PHILO T. FARNSWORTH: Interviews with Dot Debell, Elma G. Farnsworth, Agnes Lindsay, and Laura Player; Albert Abramson, *The History of Television, 1880 to 1941*, 1987; Orrin Dunlap, Jr., *Radio's 100 Men of Science*, 1944; George Eckhardt, *Electronic Television*, 1936; George Everson, *The Story of Television: The Life of Philo T. Farnsworth*, 1949; Elma G. Farnsworth, *Distant Vision: Romance and Discovery on an Invisible Frontier*, 1990; Jane Morgan, *Electronics in the West: The First Fifty Years*, 1967; Jeanne Field Olson, "Philo Farnsworth: Forgotten Inventor," *Cobblestone*, Oct. 1989; Dorothy Varian, *The Inventor and the Pilot*, 1983; Frank Waldrop and Joseph Borkin, *Television: A Struggle for Power*, 1938; Mitchell Wilson, "The Strange Birth of Television," *Reader's Digest*, Feb. 1953.

JERRALD SPENCER: Interviews with Ron Klawitter, Jim McNulty, Carolyn Spencer, Jerrald Spencer; Virginia Baldwin Hick, "For Ill Inventor, the Ideas Keep Coming," *St. Louis Post-Dispatch*, April 11, 1993.

CATHY EVANS: Interviews with Polly Boggess, Eugenia Cavender, Mary Gene Dykes, Marcelle White, and Lloyd Whitener; Martha Frances Brown, "Dalton: Carpet Capital of the World," *Georgia Life*,

Winter 1977; Martha Frances Brown, "Meet the Lady Who Started Dalton's Carpet Industry," *Georgia Life*, Winter 1977; Eugenia Cavender, genealogy supplied to author; Lee Kary, "She Started Something!" *Mountain Life and Work*, Winter 1965; "Mrs. Whitener Began Tufting Industry in 1895 When She Hand-Tufted a Spread," (Dalton) Citizen, March 14, 1958; Bob Murdaugh, "Roy Evans Recalls How Aunt Pioneered Bedspread Industry," *Dalton Advertiser*, date unknown; "Our Heritage, the Carpet Industry," supplement in *Daily Citizen-News*, Dalton, Georgia, April 25, 1993; Wyny Folk St. John, "Georgia Bedspreads Cover the Country," *Atlanta Journal Sunday Magazine*, date unknown; Autumn Stanley, *Mothers and Daughters of Invention*, 1993; Tufted Textile Manufacturers Association, "Her Little Needle Started It All," brochure; Cathy Evans Whitener, typescript of a talk given at a Dalton-Whitfield school, late fifties or early sixties; Cheryl Rose Wykoff, "A Bedspread Sampler," brochure published by the Whitfield–Murray Historical Society, 1989.

FRANK W. EPPERSON: Interview with John Epperson; Frank Epperson's family papers, genealogical materials, and reminiscences; Herb Caen, "It Takes All Kinds," *San Francisco Chronicle*, Jan. 18, 1979; George Epperson, "Popsicle—That's My Pop!" (unpublished article); Keith Power, "Meet the Popsicle Inventor," *San Francisco Chronicle*, Aug. 31, 1971; promotional materials from Popsicle Corporation, Popsicle Industries, and Gold Bond–Good Humor Ice Cream; trademark records from Gold Bond–Good Humor Ice Cream.

THOMAS EDISON: Robert Conot, *A Streak of Luck*, 1979; Thomas Edison, *The Diary and Sundry Observations of Thomas Alva Edison*, 1968, ed. Dagobert D. Runes, and *The Papers of Thomas A. Edison: The Making of an Inventor*, ed. Reese V. Jenkins et al., Feb. 1847–June 1873, 1989; Francis Arthur Jones, *Thomas Alva Edison: An Intimate Record*, 1924; Matthew Josephson, *Edison: A Biography*, 1959; J. B. McClure, *Thomas Alva Edison and His Inventions*, 1879; William Adams Simonds, *Edison: His Life, His Work, His Genius*, 1934.

MAURICE SCALES: Interviews with Era Gilbert, Tim Harvey, Waduda Henderson, Candace Scales, Maurice Scales, and Philip Scales; "Maurice Scales—Brother of Invention," *Ebony*, Oct. 1987.

BENJAMIN FRANKLIN: Benjamin Franklin, *The Autobiography and Other Writings*, ed. L. Jesse Lemisch, 1961; A. B. Tourtellot, *Benjamin Franklin: The Shaping of Genius, The Boston Years*; Mason Locke Weems, *The Life of Benjamin Franklin with Many Choice Anecdotes and Admirable Sayings of this Great Man*, 1815.

HANNAH CANNON: Interviews with Bill Cannon and Hannah Cannon; "For 12-Year-Old Hannah Cannon, Wordz Are All in the Cardz," *People Magazine*, Aug. 1988; Hope MacLeod, "Toy Biz Is Child's Play for Savvy 13-Year-Old," *New York Post*, Feb. 19, 1990.

ROBERT GODDARD: *Engineers and Inventors*, ed. David Abbott, 1986; Robert Goddard, *The Papers of Robert H. Goddard*, ed. Esther C. Goddard, vol. 1: 1898–1924, 1970; Milton Lehman, *This High Man: The Life of Robert H. Goddard*, 1963; Shirley Thomas, *Men of Space*, vol. 1, 1960; Charles Spain Verral, *Rocket Genius*, 1965.

RALPH SAMUELSON: Interview with Don Cullimore (editor and publisher of *The Water Skiier*); American Water Ski Association, "Fifty Years of Water Skiing" (program for the 1972 Championship); Jim Harmon, "The Dashing, Splashing Father of Waterskiing," *Sports Illustrated*, Aug. 10, 1987; Minnesota Department of Economic Development, "Father of Water Skiing to Represent Minnesota at Boat and Sports Shows," news release, 1972.

MARY SPAETH: Interviews with Tom Dietrich and Mary Spaeth; Kenneth Brown, *Inventors at Work: Interviews with Sixteen Notable American Inventors*, 1988; Ethlie Ann Vare and Greg Ptacek, *Mothers of Invention*, 1988.

GEORGE WESTINGHOUSE: Montrew Dunham, *George Westinghouse, Young Inventor*, 1963; Oliver Jensen, *The American Heritage History of Railroads in America*, 1975; *A Popular History of American Invention*, ed. Waldemar Kaempffert, vol. 2, 1924; Henry G. Prout, *A Life of George Westinghouse*, 1921; Westinghouse Electric, "Scenes from a Great Life," George Westinghouse Centennial pamphlet, 1946.

JOHNNIE APPLEBY: Edward W. Byrn, *The Progress of Invention in the Nineteenth Century*, 1970; Deering Harvester Company, "The Official Retrospective Exhibit of the Development of Harvesting Machinery," 1900; Douglas Hurt, *American Farm Tools: From Hand-Power to Steam-Power*, 1982; Cyrus McCormick, *The Century of the Reaper*, 1931; G. R. Quick and Wesley Buchele, *The Grain Harvesters*; F. B. Swingle, "Unbending Backs at Harvest Time," *Wisconsin Agriculturalist*, July 14, 1923; Edna Yost, *Modern Americans: In Science and Invention*, 1941.

AL GLOVER: Interviews with J. Barlow, Joe Betterton (of the Chrysler Corporation), Henry V. Borst, Olaf Childress, Al Glover, and Tommy Whitehead; Ira Abbott and Albert E. von Doenhoff, *Theory of Wing*

*Sections,* 1949; Ken Berger, "Inventor's Work Stays Hidden," *The Huntsville Times,* May 21, 1991; Charles G. Grey, *The History of Combat Airplanes,* 1941; Jay Loomis, "Farmboy-Turned-Inventor Now Has a Wall of Patents," *The* (Forest City, North Carolina) *Daily Courier,* March 13, 1991.

TOM BLANCHARD: Carolyn Cooper, *Shaping Invention,* 1991; Henry Howe, *Memoirs of the Most Eminent American Mechanics,* 1840; George Iles, *Leading American Inventors,* 1912; "Thomas Blanchard: The Inventor," *Harper's New Monthly Magazine,* July 1881.

BECKY SCHROEDER: Interviews with Charles Schroeder and Rebecca Schroeder; Toby Axelrod, "Patently Successful," *Ms,* April 1988; "Becky Schroeder: Night Writer," *Science News,* Nov. 8, 1974; Stacy Jones, "Girl, 13, Is Given Second Patent," *New York Times,* April 25, 1975; Farag Moussa, *Les Femmes Inventeurs Existent,* 1986; "Now Here Is Becky, Age 12, Getting Her First Patent," *Baltimore Evening Sun,* Aug. 22, 1974.

ELIHU THOMSON: W. Bernard Carlson, *Innovation as a Social Process: Elihu Thomson and the Rise of General Electric 1870–1900,* 1991; Orrin Dunlap, Jr., *Radio's 100 Men of Science,* 1944; National Academy of Sciences, *Biographical Memoirs,* vol. 21, 1941; David O. Woodbury, *Beloved Scientist: Elihu Thomson,* 1944.

MATTIE KNIGHT: Interview with Beatrice Kenner; Bill Delany, "Inventive Mind," (Newport News, Virginia) *Times-Herald,* Jan. 13, 1988; Alice Morse Earle, *Two Centuries of Costume in America,* vol. 2, 1903; "Famous as a Woman Inventor," *Boston Transcript.* Oct. 14, 1914; Patricia Ives, *Creativity and Inventions: The Genius of Afro-Americans and Women in the United States and Their Patents,* 1987; Robert Lovett, "Margaret E. Knight," *Notable American Women 1607–1950,* ed. Edward James, vol. 2, 1971; Anne L. Macdonald, *Feminine Ingenuity,* 1992; H. J. Mozans, *Woman in Science,* 1913; "She Was a Notable Woman," *Framingham Evening News,* Oct. 13, 1914; unpublished files at the Smithsonian Institution.

PICTURE CREDITS: Page 12, George Greenwood; pages 25 (left) and 31, Elma G. Farnsworth; page 36, Jerrald Spencer; page 43, Carpet and Rug Institute, Dalton, Georgia; pages 53 and 54, George Epperson; pages 73 and 74, William Cannon; page 87, American Water Ski Museum/Hall of Fame, Winter Haven, Florida; page 112, Al Glover; page 119, National Archives, Washington, D.C.; page 130, Thomson Consumer Electronics, Indianapolis, Indiana.

# INDEX